PEOPLE, PLANES & PROVIDENCE

First published in 2003 by

WOODFIELD PUBLISHING
Bognor Regis, West Sussex, England
www.woodfieldpublishing.com

ISBN 1-873203-90-X

People, Planes & Providence

IAN ROXBURGH

Woodfield

1937. The Author, kitted up for 'Air Experience'..

Contents

Buckingham Palace 1961.
The Author and wife Enid on the way to HM The Queen's Garden Party.

About the Author

Ian Roxburgh was born Scotland in 1917 and in 1937 joined the Glasgow Branch of the RAF Volunteer Reserve. He was taught to fly by Scottish Aviation Ltd at Prestwick and soon after getting his 'wings' early in 1939 became a flying instructor.

At the outbreak of war he carried on instructing, both in the UK and in Canada. On his return from Canada he entered Bomber Command and served on an operational Bomber Squadron (No.51) until V.E. Day. No.51 Squadron, in which he was a Flight Commander, was then converted to Transport Command, flying troops to and from India. This change in role involved a conversion from Halifax to Stirling bombers converted to carry passengers.

Released from the RAF in the autumn of 1946 he found civilian life was not to his liking and accepted the offer of a permanent commission in the RAF. He then completed a further eight years in the RAF, during which he served at The Central Flying School, The RAF Flying College and the Aircraft and Armament Experimental Establishment at Boscombe Down.

During his flying career he logged over 4,500 hours in the air in some 60 different types of aircraft. He was awarded the Air Force Medal and the Air Force Cross. For good measure he also received the Air Efficiency Award.

Preface

These writings resulted from my receiving, out of the blue, a letter from a schoolboy contemporary of mine who I had neither seen nor heard from for over 60 years. Dick Smith was now retired, having been Professor of Philosophy at St Andrews University. The letter referred to a holiday we had both spent at Kilmun on the shores of the Holy Loch on the River Clyde, during which we spent a lot of time together, messing about in boats. After that, although at the same school, we lost contact. He was a year senior to me. After a lapse of over 60 years for some inexplicable reason he had felt moved to seek me out and initiate an exchange of correspondence covering, to a large extent, our activities in the intervening years, especially the war years. Whilst I was in the RAF he was serving in minesweepers in the Royal Navy. Our exchange of information gave me the incentive to record some of my own experiences ... hence this book.

Ian D. Roxburgh
Crowthorne, Berkshire 2003

1. *Holidays*

For five years running from the age of six I spent the school holiday month of July with my family at Macharioch farm in the Mull of Kintyre. My mother and three sisters full time, my father at weekends and sometimes during the week, when he could get away from his business. The farm was near Southend and only a mile from the sea. It was an active dairy farm with a herd of about one hundred Ayrshire cows and, of course, a bull. The main product was Dunlop cheese and my sisters and I quite often assisted in its making, earnestly stirring the mixture in the huge vat. A bi-product of the cheese was the whey, which was fed to the pigs. At that stage in our young lives, living on a farm was very educational and apart from playing 'kick the can' and other simple pastimes such as 'walking on a barrel' we became aware of various aspects of nature (I well remember watching the visiting stallion doing his duty with one of my favourite mares!).

We bathed almost daily in the nearby Atlantic. The sea was sometimes so rough that my mother took the precaution of letting us into the waves one at a time whilst holding onto a rope which was tied around our waists.

One evening when walking through the field in which the herd of cows was grazing, accompanied by my two elder sisters, the bull began to behave in a strangely aggressive manner and I most ungallantly took flight and raced for the nearest fence, over which I leapt into a bed of nettles, severely stinging my bare legs. In the event my running for cover attracted the bull in my direction and my sisters were saved from any further threat!

After our five Macharioch holidays we spent our summer holidays in Arran, sometimes at Machrie Bay and sometimes at Corrie. Our main activity at both places was golf. The Machrie Bay course of nine holes had no bunkers, the natural hazards such as dry dykes, heather and natural water being more than adequate substitutes. On some days we played fifty-four holes. The course at Corrie was much more sophisticated and quite mountainous – thirty six holes per day was the maximum.

I played most of my golf at Corrie with Betty Ayton. She was the daughter of a tea-planter in Assam, where she had spent short periods of her life – sufficient to learn to count in Urdu – consequently Urdu was the language we used when counting our golf strokes from 1 to 10 (*eck, doh, ten, cha, sat, at noy, doss*). I think I was in love – puppy love – with Betty. About forty years later I bumped into a tea planter who knew the Aytons. He told me that Betty had married a British official in Assam but sad to say he had attempted to murder Betty and the resultant enquiries revealed that his first wife, who had died in unexplained circumstances, had in fact been murdered by her husband!

During my holidays I often went on fishing expeditions with my father, who was a very keen angler, sometimes joining him for a whole day's fishing on various Scottish lochs. I was the boatman and learned to make absolutely no noise in the boat whilst holding it side-on to the wind and 'drifting' over promising stretches of the loch. On one occasion whilst fishing for trout on Loch Eck (not far from the Holy Loch), a friend of my father, Ian Wood, who was fishing from the bow of the rowing boat – my father was in the stern – hooked an unexpectedly big fish which, when it leapt from the water, was a salmon of considerable size and much heavier than our light tackle could withstand. This meant that we had to give the salmon its head and follow it on a very light rein. After two and a half hours rowing up and down the loch through weeds and other hazards we finally coaxed the fish to the stern where my father gaffed it and hauled it aboard. It had been a fair fight – the fish weighed 12½ pounds and our tackle had a breaking strain of four pounds. Upon my return to school I wrote an essay about this holiday event and got a grade 'A' mark.

Whereas Corrie and Machrie were delightful places to spend a holiday, the Island capital Brodick offered rather more sophistication. The big attraction for me was the Saturday Dance at the Brodick Tennis Club. Brodick is about six miles distant from Corrie and about twelve miles from Machrie. The cycle ride from Corrie was on the level but from Machrie involved quite a climb and then descent over 'the string road' and the journey home after a night's dancing was sometimes rather testing – especially after a day's golf.

The last time we holidayed in Machrie a school friend – Gutsy Young – was also there with his family and at the end of our time at Corrie, Gutsy and I decided to spend a week at Macharioch farm. We set off on our bikes, heavily laden with tents, billycans, ground sheets and the like, heading for Loch Ranza, where we joined the boat for Cambeltown and thence to Macharioch, where we camped for a happy but quite uneventful week.

At the end of the week we struck camp and set off on the 150-mile journey back to Glasgow. Very soon after our start for home we had the first of our punctures, but we were used to repairing punctures on our well-worn tyres and not much time was lost. By the time we reached Tarbet, Loch Fyne, Gutsy had lost enthusiasm and elected to take the steamer to Rothesay, where his aunt or granny or some-such lived. We redistributed our camping equipment so that I had a full complement and went our separate ways.

On reaching Inverary at about 6pm it was still daylight so I carried on and got over 'Rest and be Thankful' – a famously steep and winding pass through the mountains – just as it was getting dark. Here, I must confess, I found the thought of camping on my own too frightening and so continued down Loch Lomond side in darkness. By this time my bike, which had been bought second-hand when already nearing the end of its life, more or less collapsed. Whilst going over Rest and be Thankful – most of which I walked up and which I fairly flew down – the spokes in the back wheel had begun to fall out. Prior to that, the leather covering on the saddle had split and the exposed springs had torn the seat of my shorts, which now barely served to conceal my rear. The bike became unrideable a few miles from Alexandria and I continued the journey as far as Alexandria on foot, pushing my seriously-damaged but much-loved bike until reaching the Police Station, where I asked for help. The police could not have been nicer and sent me on my way on the bus to Paisley, which passed the end of Dumbreck Road where we then lived. The police had kindly agreed to take care of my bike etc. By great good luck my parents were still up when I got home at about 1am and after a warm welcome was given, I tucked in to a substantial feast. The day's journey had been quite an epic, but I still had the energy to be out playing golf at ten-o-clock the next day. What it is to be young! My reward was a replacement bike complete with three-speed gear.

When my schooldays at Glasgow Academy came to an end I was very keen to see the world and with this in mind I took an office boy's job in a shipping company. But for the year or so that I had this job, none of the company's ships, all oil tankers, sailed from their long-term moorings – there must have been some sort of embargo in force – and so my world travel hopes were dashed.

Then my rich uncle invited me to join his firm, a wholesale business. I was to be schooled for management. My first few months were spent adding up columns of figures in 'day ledgers'. After being attached to various departments the day came when I was made a travelling salesman, a job which I enjoyed. In the meantime, having spent three years in the Officer Training Corps (OTC) I was invited to take a commission in the Territorial Army. Luckily I discovered from some of my school pals that there also existed the Royal Air Force Volunteer Reserve (RAFVR). This appealed to me greatly – the OTC had left me uninspired – and so, aged 20, I joined up with several of my school peers and became a Sergeant Pilot. Odd that we should be called 'pilots' considering that we had not yet flown in an aeroplane!

2.   *The RAFVR*

Joining the RAFVR was dependent upon two main qualifications: good education (in Scotland the Higher Leaving Certificate) and good health. In my case, I did not sit the H.L.C., exams because I broke my arm just before they began; luckily the authorities believed that I would have passed and I was given an honorary certification. The medical exam went well. I had been warned about a test involving blowing up a column of mercury to a certain level and holding it for as long as possible. Being prepared for this, at great effort I held up the mercury for two minutes. (I learned later that one minute would have been sufficient and bore this in mind for my future periodic medicals!)

The Ground School was a rather dingy office in Glasgow and the Flying School was at Prestwick. We attended Ground School one evening a week and spent the weekends at Prestwick. The subjects at Ground School included airmanship, internal combustion engines, compass swinging, machine gun stoppages, navigation and others. One of the airmanship lessons covered forced landings and a useful tip was that cattle always stand with their backs to the wind.

On reporting to Prestwick we were issued with our flying kit, which included a Sidcot (a one piece overall with a removable woolly lining), helmet, goggles, gauntlets and flying boots. We were introduced to parachutes with the usual jocular reminder, "if your parachute doesn't open, bring it back and you will be issued with a replacement".

My flying instructor was Mr 'Pants' Underhill, a retired Warrant Officer and a superb pilot. He took me on my first flight on a miserable November day and I will never forget the wondrous sight of the blue sky above the purest white clouds when we had climbed out of the gloomy earthbound weather. Flying in clear skies above and through towering white clouds never ceased to be a delight to me; racing along the top of a lair of cloud gives a marvellous sense of speed.

I knew at once that I was going to love flying, but it took a long time to get going. Some weekends I got only 20 minutes instruction in the air. I see from my logbook that I made my first flight on 21st November 1937 and my first solo on 20th February 1938 after 8 hours 45 minutes dual instruction – round about the average time to go solo. Things speeded up thereafter and by June 1938 I had completed over 60 hours; 32 hours 25 minutes of them solo. These hours had all been spent in a Tiger Moth, the much-loved basic trainer, but now it was time to move up to the Hawker Hart.

This was a major step; at the time the Hart Variants were still being used in operational roles. It was a most exhilarating flying machine, designed by Sir Sidney Cam, who I was to meet years later when he was in charge of the design of the Hawker Harrier – the first vertical take off and landing (VTOL) aircraft to go into full production.

Being converted onto the Hart Variants meant that most flying was solo and the accumulation of flying hours much faster. It was truly exciting flying the Hart, considered by all who flew it to be possibly the nicest aircraft ever built. It was capable of flying higher than most and looking back it surprises me that one of the exercises was a 'height test', which required one to climb as high as possible. In the Hart this was about 17,000 feet! To do this without oxygen, as we did, would not be contemplated in the RAF nowadays.

There was great excitement at Prestwick when one day a Fairey Battle arrived on the airfield. This was the first front-line monoplane to be at our disposal. Although pleasant enough as a flying machine, it was heavy and sluggish to control and really not much fun to fly. The Battle was one of the first aircraft to go into action after the outbreak of war, but possibly because of its flying qualities, it was lost in such numbers that it was very quickly withdrawn from its bombing role.

One Saturday morning in May 1939 a very strong westerly wind was blowing, but I was thought to be competent enough to fly in such marginal conditions. Landing back at Prestwick I took care to keep taxiing into wind until reaching the shelter of the wall bounding the west side of the Orange Field Hotel, which adjoined the airfield. I stayed put until, as I had expected, two of the ever-reliable ground crew came to assist me by holding onto each wingtip and so enabling me to turn across wind and taxi back to the hangars. But I had underestimated the strength of the wind, for on reaching the end of the sheltering wall it blew away the noble crewmen and the Hart finished on its nose with its wooden propeller shattered. I was helped down from my elevated position and, feeling somewhat embarrassed, made my way to the crew room. As I feared, within minutes I was summoned to the office of the Chief Flying Instructor, Flight Lieutenant Capper but on entering his office was completely taken aback when he asked me if I would undertake a flying instructor's course and on qualifying join the staff of Scottish Aviation.

I referred the CFI to the sorry sight of my Hawker Hart sitting up on its nose, but being a sensible chap he brushed it off as being 'just one of those things'. So within a few days I was sent over to our newly-completed sister airfield at Grangemouth for a somewhat sketchy four-week course (the standard RAF instructor's course took six months). On completing the four weeks I reported to RAF Upavon, then home to the Central Flying School – the very font of flying. The CFS test went satisfactorily and I started my new career as a flying instructor.

I have no doubt that it was this which led to my surviving the war. Even so, only one of my three fellow VR flying instructors lived to see the end of the war. On the outbreak of war all my fellow VRs were mobilised and posted to various assignments. A few, like me, were not required to wear sergeant's uniform and, more importantly, were kept on the Scottish Aviation payroll. This meant that instead of a Sergeant Pilot's pay of twelve shillings and sixpence per day we continued to be paid at the rate of about £800 a year. This, of course, could not last, and one by one we were posted to RAF units.

My posting came at the end of 1940 and was to RAF North Luffenham in Rutland, a brand new RAF station where I carried on instructing and soon afterwards was commissioned. At the same time, much to my delight, I was awarded the Air Force Medal, I think for my 'devotion to duty' at Prestwick.

Leaving Prestwick was a very big event for me. I had spent some three years working and playing with many friends and people I greatly admired. Moreover, I was still within reach of my many friends in Glasgow and, of course, my family. In my last few months in Scotland I had been best man at two weddings and had even been engaged for a short time –quite a common reaction to the outbreak of war. Luckily I caught 'flu' during my short engagement, which enabled both parties to realise that they had been a bit carried away by the emotional effect of the war. We remained 'just friends'.

There were, of course, many incidents and escapades during our days at Prestwick, but the fun really started in the early days of the war. On September 5th 1939, Noel Capper, by then a Squadron Leader, arrived at Prestwick in a huge aeroplane. It was the first of three Fokker passenger aircraft which Scottish Aviation had purchased in Holland to be used in the training of navigators. Avro Ansons had been used in this role up until then. (I was occasionally engaged in flying these trainee navigators as a break from flying Tiger Moths). The Fokkers were converted into flying classrooms carrying 30 students – the Ansons could only comfortably accommodate two. It was really quite an amusing sight to see thirty students being marched to the tarmac with their instructors and setting off for two hours of airborne instruction.

These aircraft were manned by a captain and co-pilot and were doing well until one day pilots David Young and 'Sausage' Palethorpe failed to notice during take-off that only three of the four engines were producing full power until it was too late to stop. It was also too late to avoid running beyond the airfield boundary and ending up forming a bridge over the Pow burn. The front end of the Fokker penetrated a wooded area which was home to a flock of hens which were seriously disturbed and shed many feathers. The wings of the aircraft were sheared off by the trees and soon after coming to rest the wreckage caught fire. Fortunately no one was seriously hurt, the worst damage being done to those who opted to jump out of the windows to the safety of the river some 10 feet below; being only six inches deep it did little to break their fall.

David McIntyre, the managing director, was probably the most seriously hurt at the loss of what, no doubt, was a highly profit-making aircraft. All three Fokkers were written off in accidents. One flew into Goat Fell, the highest mountain in Arran, but I did not get the details about the fate of the third.

The said David Young, who helped me through my instructor's course, went on to become a most distinguished bomber pilot, winning the DSO, DFC and AFC. By great good fortune I met him again in 1944, when he was my Station Commander. After the war Group Captain David Young returned to Ayrshire where he obtained the franchise for selling ice cream from kiosks along the coast. He finally retired and settled in Buckinghamshire.

An indication that we were actually at war came when all pilots were issued with a revolver and 12 rounds of ammunition. This was at a time when there was a threat of invasion by German parachutists and we were briefed to land and capture such intruders. In the event we were never faced with this exciting possibility.

During this period I was taken to court in Ayr for failing to immobilise my motorbike;[1] I had left it unattended by the beach at Troon between the hours of midnight and 1a.m. Complying with my orders to carry my revolver at all times, I arrived at court armed with my loaded revolver in my belt. No one thought of disarming me when I was sitting in the dock. My fine was 10 shillings.

Another indication that we were at war was the instruction that when we were flying our Ansons on navigation exercises over the sea we were to keep an eye open for submarines and to carry flare cartridges of the 'colour of the day' in case of being fired on by the Royal Navy. It really got serious when our Tiger Moths were fitted with bomb racks for carrying two 100-pound bombs. The plan was that we should take part in deterring the landing of troops from enemy barges. The proposed tactic was that we would

---

[1] As a wartime security measure there was a law in force that all vehicles had to be immobilised – usually by removing the rotor arm from the distributor.

sneak along the coastline at sea level and, on sighting enemy barges, 'zoom' up to a thousand feet and dive-bomb
the would-be invaders. Thank goodness we were never
called upon to do this – it would have taken at least a full
minute to 'zoom' to a thousand feet!

An interesting training exercise was 'restarting the engine in flight'. To do this, of course, it was necessary to first
stop the engine. This was not easy, because to get the propeller to stop wind-milling meant stalling the aircraft
carefully, allowing the propeller to stop rotating before the
nose dropped. The restart was achieved by diving until a
speed was reached at which the propeller would start wind-
milling. A restart was not guaranteed by this method and
there was no back-up of an electric starter, so this manoeuvre was always done within gliding range of a field into
which a forced landing could be attempted. On two occasions my engine failed to restart and I was forced to land in
the pre-selected field. On no other occasion was I faced
with the need to make a 'dead stick' landing. Incidentally,
landing in fields to collect mushrooms was a common
practise around Prestwick.

Safely up in Scotland, we were always greatly interested
when we got visits from our fellow VRs who had truly been
in action, some wearing DFC or DFM ribbons. On one
occasion one of my chums arrived in his Blenheim and
took me for a joy ride. We were also getting the sad news
every now and then of those who had been lost in action. It
was in June 1940 that we learned of France falling to the
Germans, but we all seemed to take this very calmly and

got on with the job. I think we have Winston Churchill to thank for maintaining our high morale.

On at least two occasions, fighter squadrons made re-fuelling stops at Prestwick when re-positioning from north to south or vice-versa. One of these was a Spitfire squadron and we were so pleased and comforted to see several American pilots were included. Unfortunately, two of the Spitfires made poor landings and ended up-side down. On another occasion a Hurricane squadron arrived and stayed long enough for me to persuade one of the pilots to let me have a flight in his Hurricane – another Sidney Cam master-piece. I truly enjoyed my flight in a front-line fighter aircraft but I could easily have come to grief because I failed to tighten the friction nut on the variable pitch propeller – a feature with which I was not acquainted. The result was that the propeller went into coarse pitch, which considerably extended my take-off run. Such carelessness can lead to serious trouble…

Prestwick had been a wonderful place to make a contribution in wartime. It was also most productive. Each student got about 25 hours dual instruction and each instructor did about 600 hours instructing a year; there were some 30 instructors so between them must have trained about 700 fledgling pilots per year. In addition, Prestwick produced many navigators.

Finally the day came for me to leave for North Luffenham and although looking forward to serving on a genuine RAF Station, it was a wrench leaving Prestwick and all my friends. It was, by then, the end of 1940.

3. An RAF Station

Life on an RAF Station was, of course, much more regimented than the life I had been used to. There were duties to perform, such as Orderly Officer attending Church Parades and others. These did not interfere too much with the main task, which was the training of pilots. I found living in the officers' mess most congenial but found the predominately English residents slightly strange when compared with my Scottish friends.

The most significant happening at North Luffenham as far as I was concerned was my meeting Enid Leatherbarrow, which came about as a result of a block invitation from a nearby Red Cross Hospital (Burley on the Hill, Oakham) for six officers to attend a cocktail party being given by the nurses. I was one of the lucky six and soon after arriving at the party I met a lovely young nurse, looking very clinical in her nurse's uniform and sensible shoes – but her black stocking'd ankles were a clue that other qualities were concealed beneath her strict attire. I was daring enough to invite this new-found beauty to join me on a pub visit after the party. My suggestion was gracefully accepted and Enid went off to change and reappeared in a very becoming dress and feminine shoes. To cut a long story short, after a gap of five years we met again and were married soon afterwards. We now have three children and eleven grandchildren!

I think the only other happening of note whilst I was at North Luffenham was a visit by one of my Prestwick pals, who turned up in a Manchester bomber, complete with DFM and took me for a joy-ride.

In mid summer of 1941 we vacated Luffenham to make way for a Manchester bomber squadron. The Manchester was a very disappointing aeroplane and was quickly withdrawn from service. Following considerable modification and the addition of two more engines, it reappeared as the Lancaster, the most successful bomber aircraft of its day. Sadly, before the Manchester was withdrawn, a crew made up of the Station Commander and the Squadron Section Leaders was lost with all on board. From then on crews made up of more than one Section Leader were forbidden.

My flying school was re-housed at RAF Peterborough, one of the very early RAF stations. One of the great features was the quality of the officers mess staff – all retainers of long standing. Imagine my delight at getting my morning bath run for me and my folded clothes being neatly laid out in sequence. I even witnessed my socks being sniffed to establish their suitability for another day's wear! The whole atmosphere was steeped in the best traditions of the RAF.

I wasn't at Peterborough for very long but did have some excitement there. I had a narrow squeak when I collided with another Tiger Moth whilst indulging in a mock dog-fight. During a steep turn, with my view restricted by the upper wing, I was horrified to see the other aircraft right in front, too close to avoid clipping its tail with my propeller. A large chunk of my propeller broke off and the vibration was such that I ordered my pupil to undo his straps and be ready to bail out. However, it soon became clear that the aircraft was controllable and we landed safely at our airfield. Meanwhile, I had seen the other aircraft making for home with long streams of aircraft parts trailing behind. We landed side by side and to my embarrassment I found the sole occupant was not, as I had assumed, a fellow instructor on a post-repair air test, but one of my own pupils on a solo training exercise. He had been breaking the rules by flying above solid cloud and taking part in dog fights. The ground crew repaired both aircraft in record time without any formal reporting and I worried for about three days, expecting at least a severe reprimand, but thankfully nobody bothered to take any action. I am afraid, however, that I gave my errant pupil a very severe ticking off.

Another incident was a bail out by an instructor following catastrophic technical failure. He alighted undamaged on the railway track adjoining the aerodrome.

Peterborough was a grass airfield with no runways. When the wind was too light to extend the windsock, a white wooden 'Landing T' was displayed in the 'signals square' in front of the control tower to dictate the landing and take off direction. On one occasion, one of my pupils landed in the wrong direction, causing some confusion, but fortunately no collisions. To underline the seriousness of his blunder I ordered the pupil to push the landing tee (which could be wheeled like a barrow but was rather heavy) for 100 yards along the perimeter track when flying had ceased for the day. (I do hope I was justified; even now thinking about it I feel that I was a right sod!)

Another of my Peterborough pupils, an army officer, showed his gratitude to me on a trip to London at his expense. A wealthy young man, he booked us in at the Savoy Hotel, where we were joined by his rather lovely girlfriend and very glamorous sister. We had a terrific night out, ending up at a night club in Regent Street called 'The Nuthouse'.

On returning to the Savoy, I with my Scottish Presbyterian upbringing was quite disturbed to find that the sister and I were to share a suite. London was certainly a dangerous and exciting place for rest and recreation!

Not long afterwards I was back in London to attend an investiture where King George pinned on my AFM. My parents had come down from Glasgow for the occasion (on a railway warrant supplied by HMG) and we all stayed at the Cumberland Hotel. Sir William Cooper, a business associate of my father's who had an apartment at Claridges, took us to dinner and then bridge. I partnered my father, who tended to be rather impatient when playing bridge, but on this occasion when I trumped his ace (we had been imbibing quite freely during the evening) he was uncharacteristically understanding and quite kindly suggested it was time for us to return to the Cumberland, where we bid each other good night and retired to our rooms. It was about midnight, which occurred to me to be just about the right time for a visit to the Nuthouse. Not long after arriving there I met a rather attractive girl, who in due course invited me to her flat for coffee. It seemed to me that these young society girls were really 'doing their bit for the war effort' by being very kind to stray serving men. I got back to the Cumberland in time to have breakfast with my parents, who apologised for what they felt must have been a very dull evening. I felt it discreet not to say that it really had not been at all dull!

Noel Capper (now a Wing Commander) popped in to see me one day. He arrived in a Walrus. The Walrus was an amphibious aircraft with a boat-like fuselage and landing wheels which looked like an afterthought attached to the side. The engine and propeller were stuck on behind the wings and so the aircraft was pushed along rather than pulled. It was used mainly to rescue aircrew brought down in the sea and although I can't' remember for sure I think "Cap" must at that time have been on Air-Sea Rescue duties. These unexpected visits were so welcome and emphasised that we belonged to a unique club with excellent transport facilities.

We flying instructors, although enjoying our job and undoubtedly usefully employed, felt uneasy about being remote from the business of facing the enemy and were (with some trepidation) keen to get into operational flying. It was this which induced me to visit George Reid, an ex-Prestwick pilot, who I had learned was forming a new night fighter squadron at Cranfield. George was looking for pilots and agreed to put in a request for me to join his squadron. Whilst waiting for my hoped for posting I was posted to Canada as a member of a new flying school to be opened in

Saskatchewan. I cannot deny that I was somewhat relieved and at the same time thrilled at the prospect of a visit to Canada. So on Christmas Eve 1941, along with many others who were to join the same unit as me, I boarded the good ship *Bergensfjord* at Greenock, bound for Halifax Nova Scotia.

4.   A Sea Voyage

The *Bergensfjord* was a Norwegian ship manned by Norwegians. She accommodated about two thousand troops below deck and about fifty cabin passengers. There must have been a huge larder, for we ate four substantial means a day – quite a challenge, though it must be said we service people suffered very little from food rationing at home. For the first two days we were escorted by two destroyers but thereafter we were accompanied by only one ship, which was taking German and other foreign detainees to Canadian holding units. The routine was simple, much time being devoted to eating the delicious Norwegian meals and in the evenings imbibing more than enough alcohol (at a cost of only a few shillings). There were about thirty RAF officers aboard and twelve wives en route to join their husbands somewhere in North America. The wives seemed rather a dowdy lot, but after three days at sea they became quite attractive and by the end of the 10 days voyage were almost irresistible! About half way across the Atlantic our companion ship suffered some engine trouble and we spent 24 hours circling while repairs were being made. This was a nasty period during which we on the *Bergensfjord* felt dangerously exposed. Three times during the voyage I was 'Duty Officer' – one of the duties being to accompany the Captain on his daily inspection. This included a visit below decks where some two thousand airmen were quartered. Many of them were quite ill and some must have been hoping to die as they lay on the deck with vomit rolling back and forth over their retching bodies. Never once did I feel the slightest twinge of sickness – what a bit of luck! Two days out from the Canadian coast we saw our first aircraft – friendly thank goodness – and the morale aboard rose sharply. We arrived safe and sound at Halifax early in January 1942. The *Bergensfjord* was sunk a few trips later.

As soon as we landed in Canada we boarded a train for Moncton, New Brunswick. The train journey, which began in the early evening, was enchanting, there being no 'black-out' in force as there was in Britain at the time; there were lights galore and brightly-lit Christmas trees in most kitchen windows. Moncton was a holding station and on arrival we were told to expect to be there for a week or so whilst our final destination, Assiniboia, Saskatchewan was being made ready for our occupation. In the event we spent two weeks in Moncton, making some quite warm friendships there and enjoying the luxury of shopping in stores bulging with stock.

Our next stop, after three days on a train, was Brandon Manitoba, where we were guests of the Royal Canadian Artillery, once again to await the completion of RAF Assiniboia. We stayed three weeks at Brandon, during which I spent a happy weekend at the Winnipeg home of one of the Canadian officers. His father, who was a dentist, was also the organist at the Presbyterian church and his two attractive teenage sisters sang in the choir. The night of my arrival in Winnipeg was Burns Night and I was taken to the Burns Supper by the two men of the family (the only Burns Supper I have ever attended). It was quite a night out and we got home in the early hours, tired but happy. The next morning my officer friend and I were co-opted into the church choir, which must surely have given a lot of pleasure to the congregation! After the service, the males retired to the vestry and there was a nasty moment when the organist ushered me into a WC cubicle, but to my relief this was merely to offer me a drink from his hip flask!

We were invited to visit an RCAF base where I was delighted to get back into the air again in a Cessna Crane – a twin-engined trainer very similar to an Airspeed Oxford.

At the end of our three-week stay at Brandon we were given a farewell 'dining out' party and the colonel in his address said that whereas he had been pleased to welcome the RAF to his camp, he would be reluctant to repeat the experience because of the disruption our presence had caused to his normally quiet and sober routine!

Two more days aboard a train got us to Assiniboia. The train journey of about three thousand miles across Canada was, of course, a wonderful experience. The days passed surprisingly quickly and were spent reading, playing cards – mostly poker – and looking out of the windows. In fact the views were rather disappointing. January is not the best time for such a journey because much of the weather is dull and misty and frequently snowing. For the entire journey the country was covered in snow. The train never seemed to be in a hurry and I don't think ever exceeded 40 mph. The gradients were very gentle and so we were never aware of climbing or descending. We saw many canyons and forests and lakes but not clearly because of misted up windows. The train was very comfortable, the porters being adept at converting the carriages from lounges to bunk rooms. The ablutions were adequate but did not have showers or baths. The food was first class. As far as I can remember there was no alcohol on board, there were certainly no bars.

We arrived at Assiniboia in the middle of February. It was snowbound, flat and featureless and we were at first somewhat disillusioned, having heard about the scenic grandeur of Western Canada. The prairies are far from scenic and the town of Assiniboia, with 2,000 inhabitants, was not a pretty sight; one main street with a motley collection of wooden buildings, some looking very drab. We were soon to find out, however, that the kindness and hospitality of townsfolk more than made up for the unimpressive environment. It was a happy town.

On stepping down from the train onto the packed snow, we were taken to our aerodrome, 10 miles from the town, by bus. The camp was far from complete and we had to put up with very basic conditions initially. This relative hardship served well to weld together a very happy unit. After a short time, funds became available for acquiring amenities, such as, a dartboard, a radiogram and a piano. We were then able to invite the friends we had already made in the town to the first of many mess parties.

It took several weeks for the airfield to be in a fit state for the reception of our aircraft – Tiger Moths. These had to be collected from Calgary, Alberta. Calgary lies close to the foothills of the Rocky Mountains and from here we saw our first sight of the true grandeur of Western Canada. Small groups of us went to Calgary by train, spent a few sophisticated days enjoying the town's many amenities and ferried our aircraft back to our base, stopping at Medicine Hat, Swift Current and Moosejaw (wonderful place names don't you think?) to refuel.

Usually five or six Tiger Moths were collected at a time and made the journey in loose formation. On one occasion, halfway from Calgary to Swift Current, the canopy on one of the aircraft slid back and jammed open. Pilot Officer Clark was the occupant and he had little option but to fly on the remaining 40 miles or so to Swift Current exposed to the elements. He was so frozen when he landed that he had to be helped out of the cockpit and taken to sick quarters to be thawed out. We had to leave him behind, but he turned up later, fully-recovered, having joined the next batch of aircraft to come through.

Navigation was simple on cross country flights, made easy by the clearly visible North/South boundaries of the huge wheat fields, even when covered with snow. It was simply a case of using the compass to establish the angle at which to cross the fields and then pressing on. Map reading was of little use in the featureless prairie, all the small towns being many miles apart. The only landmarks were the grain elevators which could be seen from time to time standing high against the horizon alongside the Canadian Pacific

Railway line which ran east-to-west well to the south of our track. We had no radio so all flights were 'contact'.

The Canadian Tiger Moths were quite different to the UK versions in that they had perspex hoods, heaters, tail wheels and brakes. There were, therefore, comparatively sluggish, particularly because our airfield was three thousand feet above sea level.

Our first batch of students arrived from the UK – thirty of them. First impressions were that they looked, en masse, most unpromising. However, they soon developed into interesting individuals, most of whom passed the course and went on to goodness-knows-what achievements.

The routine was simple and our leisure time was spent either shooting gophers or with friends in Assiniboia. The gopher shooting was so extensive that after a few weeks no gophers were to be seen within about three miles of the base. Out Station Commander, Wing Commander Lee Cox, did not disapprove of the massacre, although he did not join in. Instead he preferred to photograph the gophers, the only form of wildlife we ever saw. He went to a lot of trouble, concealing himself beside the gopher holes, awaiting the emergence of a family group and more than once being frustrated by the whine of a .22 bullet leaving only one (deceased) member of the family on view!

To relieve the congestion at our base, a relief landing ground was prepared some ten miles distant. Whilst operating from this we experienced our first 'line squall'. A line squall is a very clearly defined frontal system stretching for several miles, which rushes across the country at some 70 mph, causing great havoc. This high wind was more than our Tiger Moths could stand and those that were on the ground simply blew away and those that were airborne hightailed away down wind and landed in odd places miles from home. One exception was Pilot Officer Jepps, who daringly flew into the teeth of the storm and emerged about 20 minutes later to find that he had hardly moved relative to the ground, his airspeed having matched very closely the windspeed he was heading directly into.

We were left with very few serviceable aircraft but none were too seriously damaged.

5. Canada

I am sorry to say that, as so often happened, on being posted to Arnprior – a flying instructors' school in Ontario, I lost touch with my Assiniboia friends. News did reach me about one of my colleagues to whom I had sold my car for 25 dollars – an ageing Hupmobile – which had done me well. The purchaser did not have the funds for me on the spot but promised to send on the payment as soon as he could. By sheer bad luck, a few days after I left, he was driving along the dirt road to Assiniboia when the engine fell away from the chassis … so I did not get my 25 dollars.

Much later I learned that one of my best friends there, George Mosley, who came from the Bahamas, had been killed in the Middle East. He, like one of my old Prestwick pals, George Norton, had been lost when making an attack in their American-made Kittyhawk fighters.

I quite recently discovered that one of my golfing friends was a student pilot whilst we were both in Assiniboia. David Johns had spent a night in the local jail for some minor misdemeanour. Had I known I might have intervened on his behalf, because I was a close friend of the Sheriff's eldest daughter, Genevieve. Perhaps if I had tried it would have done more harm than good.

To my delight the Station Commander at Arnprior was Wing Commander John Stockbridge, who had been my

CO at North Luffenham. He had been joined by his wife Alice and their daughter Margaret. They lived in a house in the town of Arnprior where they gave some great parties. (I played the piano for musical chairs at Margaret's 12th birthday party.)

The students at Arnprior were nearly all Canadians and I found teaching pilots to be flying instructors very dull work. In a way I think I was ready for a change; I was beginning to feel the strain of the responsibility of sending trainee pilots on their solo flights, especially their first solo. How much longer was I going to get away without someone hurting himself?

Arnprior was within reach of some wonderful leisure opportunities. Only 40 miles from Ottawa a night out there was easy and about 100 miles to the north east were the Laurentian Mountains of Quebec, a great playground both in summer and winter. I skied there frequently, sometimes joined by Adam Bailey, who had been with me at Prestwick. We were both staying at Grey Rocks Inn, St. Jovite (Adam's wife was with him). One morning it was too windy to ski but by lunchtime the wind had eased and Adam and I set off from Grey Rocks in a pony and sleigh for a nearby mountain with many pistes. The lower lifts were not operating because of the wind, so we clambered up on foot, carrying our skis for the first 1,000 feet or so when we were in cloud. Oddly, the upper ski tow was operating and this took us up the remaining 2,000 feet. It was very murky and we felt a bit peckish and were lucky enough to come across shelter equipped with soup-making facilities. Fortified, we then sought out the beginners run to return to base but by mistake took 'Ryans Run' which was the second fastest on the mountain. Our skiing abilities were not up to this and after a hilarious forty minutes, much of it spent getting back on our skis, we reached the bottom. As I was entering the bar of the base hotel, covered in snow, a young teenage girl asked where I had been and I proudly said that I had just come down Ryans Run. "Oh," she said, "how long did you take?" I mumbled, "about a quarter of an hour," to which she responded, "Oh, I came down in three minutes yesterday."

After some drinks, Adam and I decided to leave the pony in the stable and got a lift back to Grey Rocks to find a very het-up Mrs Bailey, who not long afterwards got divorced from Adam. Years later I met Adam with a re-placement wife.

Another old colleague at Arnprior was 'Pants' Under-hill, who had been my first instructor at Prestwick. He became Chief Instructor and I became his deputy.

The proprietor of Grey Rocks Inn was Tom Wheeler. Tom was a pioneer of aviation in North America and founded Wheeler Airlines in the twenties, which provided a service between New York and Quebec. Although one of the first in the field, Tom did not develop his airline and it became little more than a Bush Flying Service, taking hunters on fishing and shooting expeditions in northern Quebec. When I was on the scene, Tom had only a few amphibious Norsemen aircraft, which he very kindly of-fered to me for commuting at weekends between St. Jovite and Arnprior. I never took advantage of this, however, because it was permissible and more convenient to use RCAF aircraft. (We had Fairchild Cornells, Fleet Finches, Tiger Moths, Boeing Stearmans and a Harvard to choose from. The Stearman was my favourite.)

I visited St Jovite in 1956 and Tom was still there, but had sold Grey Rocks and built Lacouimey Club. By this time he was operating about 20 four-engined, transport aircraft which were under contract to supply the DEW Line (the distant early warning line crossing Northern Canada). This was very lucrative and as Tom spent the day enjoying the facilities of his millionaire's club, his thoughts were concentrated on what to do with the millions of dollars which were falling into his lap. To make things even more lucrative for him, he sold his air business to one of the major airlines, just weeks before the DEW line project was cancelled. Round about the same time I called on one of his daughters, with whom I had been friendly and who, after marrying, was living in New York. She and her husband took me to a restaurant where, sitting next to us, was Henry Fonda.

Talking about film stars reminds me of a trip I made from Assiniboia to Hollywood. I went with 'Doc' Fraser ex-Glenalmond, via Greyhound bus. We spent two weeks in and around Los Angeles and had a quite splendid time. In 1942 RAF officers were lionised by the Americans and the stars of Hollywood excelled at this. One star rather let me down however, namely George Raft. I bumped into him somewhere and he took me to a night-club where we were joined by two somewhat brassy blondes. When the time came to leave, I excused myself to go to the loo and when I returned all three had disappeared – luckily the bill had been paid. However, it left me with the view that George Raft had been well cast in his gangster roles! One of my nicer memories was a visit to Nigel Bruce's home where, amongst other pleasant moments, I played gin rummy with Anne Baxter, who was then just a starlet. Doc Fraser and I had been given a letter of introduction to the owner of the Brown Derby restaurant and, typical of the hospitality of the Americans (although this chap was actually a Canadian) he insisted that the Doc and I had one meal a day at his restaurant, on the house. This resulted in us meeting lots of celebrities; we even had a meal with Shirley Temple and her parents. Shirley was only twelve, but quite lovely, and despite her fame, totally unspoilt and natural. She, as you may know, became an American Ambassador – how interesting it would be to meet her again.

6. *Back to the War*

Two years after my arrival in Canada my tour there came to an end. It had been a wonderful experience but I was not without some trepidation glad to be going back to the reality of the war. When I gave thought to the dreadful things which were going on in other parts of the world. I could not escape a sense of guilt at my good luck.

Many of my contemporaries and their families had faced huge challenges, hardships and losses. George Reid, who's Night Fighter Squadron I might have joined, was one of the missing.

My visit to Canada ended where it had begun, in Monkton, New Brunswick. My good friend and fellow instructor Peter Major and I were held there awaiting shipment back to the UK. On New Year's Eve 1943 Peter and I were getting down to celebrating the New Year when, at about 10pm, the Mess President, a Canadian Wing Commander, closed the bar. Peter and I reacted badly to this and promptly ordered a taxi to take us to a nearby RCAF Station where, to our delight, a proper New Year's Eve party was in full swing. When the party was coming to an end, Peter and I felt reluctant to go back to our dreary mess, so when we discovered that an aircraft was due to leave Monkton for New York at 2am, we decided that this was an opportunity not to be missed. We had a super few days being thoroughly spoilt in New York and were relieved to find on our return to Monkton that our absence had gone unnoticed.

We returned to New York a few days later to set sail for home in the *Isle de France* – together with about 15,000 American GIs. The voyage was not enjoyable – two meals a day and no alcohol. Luckily I had had the foresight to put six bottles of Black & White whisky in my cabin luggage. This brought me great popularity, which sadly survived only two days until the last bottle was emptied. The crossing took fourteen days, extended because frequent diversions had to be made to avoid the U-boat packs about which we were warned from time to time. When we arrived at Greenock I was very put out to be charged £1 duty on the further six bottles of whisky which had been stored in the luggage hold. To make matters worse, when I eventually opened my trunk I found that two of the bottles had broken – a loss compounded by the consequent staining of my clothing.

Back on land again we were all put on a train bound for somewhere in England, where we were immediately sent on leave. So back up to Glasgow I went, to be reunited with my family. My sister Margot was an active member of the Women's Voluntary Service and during my leave she took me on one of her trips delivering items of comfort to girls serving at various military centres. We got as far as Oban, which I thoroughly enjoyed, although I do remember feeling cold and miserable in the badly-heated buildings and the damp climate. Although the temperature I had left in Canada had been well below freezing, the atmosphere had been dry and the cold much less invasive.

While on leave in Glasgow I met an RN Captain in Rogano's – a popular restaurant in the city. We spent a pleasant hour or two at the bar and at closing time he invited me to join him on his ship, the *Ravager*, a utility aircraft carrier which was moored at Greenock. We had established that we were both keen bridge players and the idea was to finish off the evening at the card table, which we duly did. The Captain must have had his own transport because I cannot recall any difficulty in getting from Glasgow to Greenock, a journey of some 20 miles.

After our bridge game I was given a cabin for the night and to my great surprise when I woke up and looked out of the porthole it was broad daylight and we were out at sea. Soon a steward appeared with my morning tea and he was followed by my official escort – the ship's doctor. The doctor looked after me very nicely and took me up on deck, or rather onto a sort of platform which hung over the side of the ship at a height which brought ones eyes to the level of the landing deck. It was explained that this was the ideal level to watch the aircraft landings, which were due to begin any minute.

The first batch of aircraft to arrive were from nearby Machrihanish (not far from Southend, where years before I had spent my summer holidays) and were flown by newly-trained pilots; this was their first shot at landing on a real deck. I found it all very disturbing, because almost every other landing ended with a broken aeroplane, some of which were bulldozed over the side to keep things moving along. The doctor told me that this was a good average success rate and soon another batch arrived, this time flown by experienced pilots making a few practice landings before joining their operational carrier. This turned out to be even more disturbing, because two out of three landings turned out so badly that I had to ask to be taken to the wardroom without delay. We were somewhere west of Loch Ranza when it became time for me to leave and I was flown back to Ayr racecourse in an Avenger. (Years later, in the early 1950s, a batch of Avengers was brought for the Fleet Air Arm and I flew one quite often at that time in Handling Squadron.)

With my repatriation leave over I returned to my holding unit in England where I was invited to choose what I would like to do next. In truth there was very little choice: fighters or bombers. The Mosquito had captured the imagination of many pilots and most of those returning from Canada such as myself, were dead-set on getting onto a Mosquito squadron. The Mosquito was one of the most versatile of all WW2 aircraft and was used in many different roles. I was particularly keen on its night-fighter role, but on applying for this I was advised that it would be at least six months before I could expect to reach a squadron. However, it was said that I could get into the heavy bomber stream straightaway. There seemed to be no option, so onto bombers I went, despite the feeling that I was really not brave enough to face the dangers involved; listening to the reports of the feats of the bomber crews whilst enjoying the comfort and security of being in Canada had convinced me that heavy bombers were not for me.

My introduction to bombers was at Lossiemouth, where I spent two months learning the trade. Much of the flying took place at night, as you might expect, but it was mid-summer and therefore very little time was spent in darkness; I think at most two hours darkness per day was all we had. Some evenings, as my aircraft climbed out northwards from Lossiemouth, the sunsets were as beautiful as any I have ever seen anywhere in the world.

My experience stood me in good stead and my crew came out top of the course. This meant that my name was added to the propeller mounted above the mantelpiece in the Officers Mess with all the previous top performers.[2] From Lossiemouth, some weeks were spent on different courses such as Escape and Evasion, Blind Landing, and Radar Systems – ending up with a conversion course onto the Halifax. All this preparation took almost 10 months and it was not until 10th November 1944 that I joined 51 Squadron, 4 Group, Bomber Command, then based at Snaith in Yorkshire.

After one or two familiarisation flights in daylight I was, as was the custom, sent on a local night-time cross country, which was to take four hours. One other brand new crew was doing the same trip. The weather was very

---

[2] In 1946, I took my new bride to Lossiemouth to show off this record of my greatness, only to find that Lossiemouth had been taken over by the Navy and the propeller removed. Enid and I were spending a few weeks at Edzell at the time and we drove back over Cairono'mount on the 15th May in a snowstorm.

poor and had I been in authority I would not have authorised the flights. Anyway, off we went, observing, as was mandatory, radio silence until almost four hours later, we once again saw the ground on our approach to Snaith. We then learned that the other crew had crashed just a short time after take off and all had been killed.[3]

The next routine step should have been an operational flight as supernumerary member with an experienced aircrew – a sort of baptism of fire – but luckily, thanks to my experience (I had, by this time, more than 3,000 hours in my logbook whereas my fellow squadron pilots had an average of about 300 hours) I was excused this, to my mind, unnecessary risk.[4]

It is amazing to think that these very young and relatively inexperienced volunteers were able to take off in heavily-laden four-engined bombers, which by today's standards were pretty crude, fly them in darkness for an average time of 6 hours, much of it over hostile territory, drop their bombs and get back to base with the most basic of navigation aids, eventually landing by the light of 'glim lamps', barely visible from half a mile away. But they did it; and very willingly too.

---

[3] Quite recently a chap wrote to me from Yorkshire asking if I could recall that night because he had taken such an interest in the crashed aircraft and its crew that he had raised funds from local people to place a memorial stone at the place of the impact.

[4] Bill Elder, one of my fellow instructors at Prestwick was lost on his initiation flight.

Soon after joining the Squadron I was appointed Flight Commander, which meant promotion to Squadron Leader and the allocation of a motorbike. My fellow Flight Commander was John 'Plug' Lodge. He was on his third tour of ops and survived the war after completing 64 operational sorties. This was acknowledged by just one 'mention in despatches' – a poor reward indeed and I fear one of many such anomalies. John was my 'Best Man' but tragically died of pneumonia whilst still in his thirties.

So much has been written about bomber raids that I feel my experience, limited to 15 sorties, is nothing out of the ordinary. However, two events which occurred to me were somewhat unusual…

One night when I was acting Squadron Commander, I had seen off the squadron on a raid when, a few minutes after the last aircraft had disappeared into the gloom, we were surprised to get a call from 'Graceless Dog' ('Graceless' was our squadron call-sign) requesting permission to land. This caused considerable alarm because, firstly, radio silence was mandatory and secondly, D-Dog was not amongst the aircraft that had taken off; in fact, D-Dog had failed to return from the previous night's op and had not been re-placed. It was so strange that I was not the only one who wondered if it was a ghostly plane with an ethereal crew!

D-Dog landed and out stepped the crew that had taken off some 24 hours before; surely a miracle. The explanation was that D-Dog had made an emergency landing on a remote landing field in France, where there were no communications with the UK. After getting some fuel, which had taken all day to procure, the crew flew back to base. We didn't know whether to kiss them or kick them!

The other event concerned myself. I was 'stood down' and my crew sent on leave whilst I was recovering from a foot injury (caused by my falling off my motorbike). This was very near to the end of the war and the demands on Bomber Command were easing off. One lovely May morning we were briefed to attack some gun emplacements on Wangerooge, one of the Fresian Islands off Holland. Two hundred bombers were taking part and there were said to be no anti-aircraft defences on the island. One of my captains had failed to report for the briefing and this simple daylight raid on a defenceless target seemed too good to miss, so I opted to take the captain-less crew. The crew, which was fairly new to the squadron, was made up of six very tough-looking Australian sergeants. I was still using a walking stick and wearing a carpet slipper on my sore foot and these Aussies very gently helped me into my seat in the cockpit. When we approached the target, to my surprise, it was black with anti-aircraft fire right at our altitude of 8,000 feet. Moreover, we saw several aircraft going down in flames. As we went through the target, we felt a thump and my port inner engine was out of action. With this engine feathered, we were out of the danger area and over the sea in no time and all set for the journey home.

My six sergeants were terribly excited at the thought of being hit – this was their sixth trip and their first experience of flak damage. When we landed back at base they could hardly wait to get out to inspect the damage and, sure enough, there was a large hole on the underside of the port inner engine. I am sure they all dashed of to report this great experience to their chums. I never saw any of them again, luckily as it happens, because an hour after landing, while I was having a drink in the mess, my Squadron Engineer came to tell me that we had not been hit by flak after all; a piston rod had broken and the piston had shot out through the bottom of the engine, a Hercules Radial.

That was the last raid carried out by Four Group and of the two hundred aircraft taking part, thirty four were lost. It was a terrible shame, so near the end of the war and for so little purpose.

VE Day followed very soon afterwards and by way of celebration three of my chums and I decided to pay a visit to Scarborough. We had moved to Leconfield, near Beverley at this time, so Scarborough was within range of my little car, a Standard 8. Before setting off, I had taken the precaution of putting a case of beer in the boot – very luckily as it turned out.

We had a boisterous time and rendezvoused at midnight for our return to Leconfield. Somehow we got off track and found ourselves climbing up an ever-worsening road. We reached the summit just as we noticed the engine was issuing steam. We obviously needed water, but had little hope of finding any at the top of Yorkshire Moor, so we decided to use our stock of beer as a substitute.

Just in time, one of us suggested that we should drink the beer first. This we did, and waited until the beer took its natural course, then one-by-one we rather untidily topped up the radiator from our own resources!

We got home without further ado and the car seemed none the worse for the experience.

7. Targets in Germany

Apart from the last 4 Group raid on Vangerooge, all my targets were in Germany. Six of these were in daylight, the rest at night. These were amazing experiences – a mixture of excitement, apprehension and fear. On several occasions I experienced flak damage. The elation one experienced on returning safely was very marked. The average sortie time was about 6 hours, much of it with nothing to be seen except, if not in cloud, the stars. Luckily I particularly enjoyed flying in darkness and found a star-filled sky beautiful and comforting. Even the engines seemed to run more sweetly at night. There was, of course, plenty of time to reflect on one's immediate situation and my great worry was the possibility of becoming a Prisoner of War.[5]

I think it was during this time that I developed an unwillingness to form deep friendships, which I regret has persisted to this day. Although quite gregarious and very fond of good company, I find I do not wish to get involved. Postings every few months which meant a sudden end to new friendships and the loss of many old chums probably had this effect. Nevertheless, I have hundreds of kind and

---

[5] Somewhat strangely, the possibility of death did not really cause me any trouble because I had formed the firm opinion that I would go straight to heaven, where I envisaged a huge and comfortable bar where all my old mates would give me a warm welcome!

much-respected acquaintances scattered throughout the world whose friendship I very much value.

My longest raid was a nine-hour round trip to Chemnitz (Bavaria). This was an unusual raid because on arrival at Chemnitz we descended some 14,000 feet to get below cloud for a visual attack. Having dropped our bombs we then climbed away on our way home. The return cruising height was to have been 16,000 feet but because of heavy airframe icing we could not get above 10,000 feet and to stay there had to use higher power than expected and so use fuel at a higher rate. We had heard on a radio broadcast that the weather over Yorkshire and for many miles around south east England had seriously deteriorated and that the pre-planned diversions were to be used. We made for Abingdon, where we landed with very low fuel levels. There were so many diverted crews that I, along with many others, had to spend the remainder of the night sleeping on the floor of the Mess.

Strangely, no provision was made in the Halifax for calls of nature and so the arrangement I made was for my Flight Engineer, Sgt Jack Ryde, to keep a tin can on board for my use. On most flights I would need to make use of this facility, but on one occasion Jack mislaid the tin can and, sensing my desperation, elected to use the end cap from a flare as a substitute. After the usual negotiating of seal belt, parachute harness and other obstructions, I had been comfortably under way for a little while when my Wireless Operator, Warrant Officer Terry Bennett RAAF, who sat directly beneath me, reported a peculiar warm liquid spray invading his compartment. It turned out that the flare cap had perforations on the sides about an inch up from the bottom. The resultant overflow explained not only Terry's distress but also the surprisingly large capacity of my substitute receptacle!

My Navigator was Flying Officer Jim Robb RNZAF. He was a very competent officer and made only one serious navigation blunder when we were making a 'feint' attack on Harburg (nr. Hamburg). For this raid 51 Squadron was detailed to proceed at the head of the main bomber stream and at a certain point continue for a further few minutes, creating a diversion by chucking out 'window' (aluminium foil strips which simulated lots of aircraft on enemy radar screens) whilst the main stream veered off to the real target. This procedure was designed to mislead the enemy night-fighters. Having done our stuff we were then supposed to join up with the tail end of the main stream and drop our bombs.

In the event, Jim made a mistake and left our turn to join the main stream rather late. It was a clear night, enabling me to see in the distance the attack on Harburg was well under way, but despite my frequent suggestions to Jim that it was high time we changed course he insisted on holding onto his beliefs.

As a result we were ten minutes late and when we eventually made our run up to the target the raid had ended and we made our contribution all on our own. It seemed that every searchlight homed in on us, but I can only conclude that the anti-aircraft guns had put their covers on in the belief that the raid had ended, because belief that the raid had ended, because nobody fired a shot at us.

March 1ˢᵗ 1945 was the day of the Rhine crossing. We were given the task of bombing enemy targets just across the river on the east side. This attack had to be 'visual' because of the proximity of our own forces on the ground. The weather was good with low mist obscuring the ground on our approach to Cologne, our first sight of which was the beautiful twin steeples of Cologne cathedral soaring up through the mist. A year or two later I visited Cologne and was amazed to find no signs of damage to the cathedral, which seemed like a miracle considering the surrounding destruction.

It is strange that very little thought was given by the bomber crews to the destruction and distress that they were creating when dropping their bombs on the enemy cities, probably because they had enough to think about as far as their own vulnerability was concerned, coupled with the belief that they were contributing to beating Hitler and his evil regime. Just a few years ago when I was on holiday in Madeira, a German lady and her 20-year-old daughter were staying at my hotel. We had little chats from time to time and it transpired that at the age of twelve she was a resident of Chemnitz when it was bombed, not long before the war ended. She described the horror of it all, but bore me no ill will when I told her that I had taken part in that raid.

Soon after 'VE' Day we took our ground staff on sightseeing trips to Germany in our Halifax's to give them the opportunity to see at first-hand the results of Bomber

Command's efforts. The devastation was terrible and I particularly remember Hamburg, where absolutely no building appeared to be standing. A dreadful sight.

51 Squadron was rather deprived in being based at Snaith. RAF Snaith was very much a utilitarian wartime station with the minimum of facilities and in a dismal part of Yorkshire. Apart from one or two primitive pubs there were no recreations within walking distance. To make my recollections even more gloomy, the weather during the winter of 1944/45 was cold and miserable – I cannot remember ever seeing the sun.

The Officers Mess, like all other buildings, was built of wood and was very basic with rather ineffective coal fires. The admin officers were very crafty at getting to the mess early at meal times and could usually be found well established round the fire, reading the more popular newspapers. From time to time this monopolising was disturbed thanks to Flight Lieutenant Geoffrey Praill who, at appropriate opportunities, would set fire to the hand held newspapers, causing a sort of delayed but quite startling reaction. On one occasion, whilst some building was going on, Geoffrey seized the opportunity to climb onto the mess roof bearing a brick, which he dropped down the ante-room chimney and fairly scattered the administrators hogging the hearth.

Whilst he was carrying out this deed the Base Commander, Group Captain Fresson, came by and seeing Geoffrey on the roof asked, "What are you doing, Praill"?

"Dropping a brick, Sir," was the apt reply.

My 'war wound' – the injury to my foot – happened at Snaith. It occurred one exceptionally cold and frosty morning. I had been on a raid the night before and on waking up at about midday in my unheated wooden hut about 2 miles away from the mess, and with a jug of icy water provided for my ablutions, I thought, for the one and only time that I can remember, I would wear my issue 'long johns' to help me endure the motorbike ride to the mess. With our flexible working hours, the day very often started with lunch rather than breakfast. En-route I decided to divert to the ops room to have a look at the pictures taken of the previous night's target. I took a short cut along a narrow path but failed to notice a piece of angle iron jutting about 6 inches above ground. This caught my foot, which was pulled back against the bike's foot-rest and removed my toe cap and very nearly most of the toes on my right foot.

For the first time I was a patient in Sick Quarters where I was beautifully looked after, although I was slightly embarrassed at being discovered wearing long-johns, which had had to be cut off. After a few days I was able to hobble about on crutches and was allowed to be taken to the mess at teatime. Very seldom did I get back before midnight, thanks to my fellow officers showing me off at a local pub and spreading false tales about how I had been injured carrying out a most daring raid. No matter how much I protested the locals plied me with beer, which made my progress on crutches very hazardous.

On the night of one raid when I was acting Squadron Commander, I was in the Control Tower awaiting the return of my squadron when Snaith was attacked by German intruders. Such attacks were designed to shoot down the RAF bombers as they returned to their bases. Our procedure was to divert our aircraft and darken the airfield. On this night our brightly illuminated identification lights would not go out from the Central Control, so very bravely I thought, I drove across the airfield in the CO's car – a camouflaged Hillman Minx – and managed to douse the lights. Making my way back I met a crew bus looming out of the darkness. We both stopped and I got out and found a little WAAF in charge of the bus all on her own. She had some time before been despatched to an aircraft dispersal to pick up a returning crew and after sitting through a quite dramatic strafing of the airfield had decided it was time to go back for fresh instructions. She was absolutely unperturbed and I am sure it had not occurred to her she was in mortal danger; a wonderful example of the many unsung heroines of the WAAF.

Towards the end of March 1945, it was rumoured that the squadron was going to be moved and, sure enough, on 21st April we moved lock, stock and barrel to RAF Leconfield. What prompted the powers-that-be to order this move at such a late stage in the war, goodness knows, but whatever it was, it was a merciful relief to be based on a proper permanent peacetime RAF station. The comfort, the facilities and the general ambience raised our quality of life quite dramatically and, what's more, we were only a few miles from one of Yorkshire's loveliest places, the town of Beverley, and for those who liked bigger cities, Hull was only 13 miles distant. (I must confess that the only attraction I found in Hull was the Greyhound Race Course.)

Within a month of completing the move the war in Europe was over, which was followed fairly quickly with the breaking up of our bomber crews. Parting from those with whom we had shared hopes and fears for almost a year was a strange mixture of joy and sorrow. Jim Robb went home to New Zealand to resume his school-teaching; Terry Bennett to Australia from whence he wrote me a most moving and cherished letter; my bomb aimer Chris Smart, who was also vice-captain of my crew, went off to his home near London. Chris was a very fine airman and seemed to have a knack of being at the right place and doing really useful things without any prompting – he was also a most determined bomb aimer and never once wavered in keeping me on the straight and narrow during the nerve-racking runs up to the target. Jack Ryde did not have far to go, being a Yorkshireman. My two gunners were Scotsmen: 'Jock' Meldrum from Glasgow and Gillies Torrence from Elgin. The following summer I went up to Elgin to be Gillies' best man. Gillies was the rear gunner. This must have been the worst job of all in bombers. The hours spent in his lonely post hanging out of the rear of the Halifax in his cramped and cruelly cold gun turret must have tested to the limit his courage and endurance, especially considering how frequently it had to be repeated.

It was rumoured that there was one rear gunner who had suffered so much boredom that he took to carrying a torch with him with which to attract enemy night fighters.

This only came to light when an investigation was made into why this particular crew seemed to be singled out for enemy attacks and why the rear gunner was accumulating such a high score of 'kills'.

8. Goodbye to the Halifax

My last flight in a Halifax, a sight-seeing tour of Emden, Bremen and Hamburg was on 19th June 1945. In the meantime 51 Squadron had been transferred to Transport Command and our conversion onto passenger-carrying Short Stirlings had begun. When I say passenger-carrying, I should explain that the seating arrangements were primitive in the extreme – string hammocks hanging along each side of an un-insulated fuselage. No galley of course, the meals being issued in cardboard boxes placed on boards. The poor passengers, bound for India, who were in any case very reluctant to serve in the Far East, had to suffer this discomfort for eight or so hours per day for four or five consecutive days.

Going from the Halifax to the Stirling was without a doubt a retrograde step and did not go down well with either the aircrews or the ground crews. They were ungainly, difficult to maintain and awkward to fly. One characteristic was a very strong tendency to 'swing' on take-off which, if allowed to develop, caused the undercarriage to collapse – the result was that there was hardly an RAF staging post anywhere which did not have bent and broken Stirlings lying around the airfield. There were occasions when swinging aircraft crashed into buildings in the vicinity of the runway, control towers being the most vulnerable.

It was not until Geoffrey Tyson (Short's chief test pilot) spent a few days with the squadron to help us with our conversions that we discovered that – in the hands of such a super pilot – the Stirling became completely docile and manageable. Years later Geoffrey Tyson became famous for his demonstrations in the Short Saro I Flying Boat Fighter at the Farnborough Air Shows, when he would fly the length of the airfield upside down as a regular feature. By this time I had made friends with Geoffrey and we played golf together quite often until he was no longer able to play because of severe arthritis. He died in his early eighties.

Transport Command was a very new way of life and the opportunity it offered to see the world was very attractive. On my first trip, on 5th September 1945 (my 28th birthday) I set off from Stoney Cross in the New Forest, Hampshire, for Calcutta with staging-post stops at Castel Benito (Libya), Lydda (Israel), Shaiba (Iraq) Mauripur (Karachi), St Thomas (Madras), Dum-Dum, Calcutta, then returning to England across Northern India to Karachi via Alahabad. We landed back at Stoney Cross on 18th September. Almost everybody had lost at least a stone in weight, partially because of the heat, but mainly because of 'Gippy tummy'. Fortunately, we returned empty, so the constant demand for the Elsan was shared between just a few aircrew. (When I say 'empty' this does not take into account the cargo of Indian carpets we brought back to sell in England – at 300% profit!)

During the war, modifications and additions were almost continually being made to our aircraft to improve their effectiveness or to extend their use. One of these was 'Rocket Assisted Take-off'. The arrangement was to attach rockets to the wings to give extra thrust for take-off, thereby increasing the possible payload. Trials were carried out on various aircraft, including the Stirling. It was told to me that the trials on the Stirling culminated in a demonstration to lots of 'brass hats', who had assembled at a remote airfield. The Stirling had been positioned at the end of the runway and the VIPs lined up by the control tower to witness this significant breakthrough. The countdown started and in accordance with the plan, the engines roared and the rockets went off. Immediately the Stirling disappeared in great clouds of smoke – but to everyone's surprise the aircraft did not, as expected, emerge at high speed. It was not until the smoke cleared that the Stirling could again be recognised, but by this time it was minus its wings, which were now lying alongside the fuselage. This was sufficient evidence for the powers-that-be to abandon further attempts to improve the performance of the Stirling.[6]

Sir Ralph Cochrane was a very great officer and played a huge role in the development of the RAF, both in times of peace and war. Just after the war he was AOC-in-C of Transport Command and I was a Flight Commander in one of his Stirling squadrons. As I said earlier, my squadron was engaged in flying troops to and from India and quite often I would fly as supernumerary on various legs, choos-

---

[6] Some people even say that this is a true story!

ing to change aircraft and thereby crews from leg to leg; and again from choice, usually stopping in Tel Aviv for a few days – which I very much enjoyed – comparing notes with my captains as they passed through. On one occasion the Station Commander, Group Captain Morrison (whom I had previously met in Canada but did not take to), ordered one of my crews to proceed to Sharja in the Gulf, despite my captain's decision not to do so because of a wicked weather report. I instructed my captain, who had full authority to make his own decision, to disregard the Group Captain. The next day I went on to India and arrived back in England a week or two later to be told I had to report immediately to AOC-in-C (Sir Ralph himself). It was a formal enquiry into why I had defied the Group Captain. On hearing my side of the story the Group Captain was brought home and reduced to his substantive rank of Wing Commander. Fortunately, I never again came across Wing Commander Morrison.

The first airlift we did was from Brussels, taking soldiers to Karachi. Typically, the first take-off was to be at midnight. Stirlings and Liberators were taking off alternately. The first aircraft was a Stirling, which thirty or so soldiers had very reluctantly boarded (they felt they were entitled to home leave before going to the Far East). Within a few minutes from take-off the Stirling was back in the circuit with only three engines working and jettisoning fuel in order to get down to landing weight. In the meantime, under great persuasion, the next batch of thirty soldiers had boarded the first Liberator, which then took off and on reaching about 1,000 feet promptly exploded, falling to earth in smithereens. Two soldiers had refused to board the Lib and were taken to the guardroom. At their court-martial they pleaded that they had had a premonition about the accident and were set free. The remainder of the Brussels exercise ended in great confusion and several generals were called to the scene to get things sorted out.

In spite of the attractions of world-wide travel, the business of sitting in an aircraft doing 140 knots in level flight for eight hours at a stretch soon became extremely boring and quickly dispelled any illusions I might have had about joining an airline.

Early in January 1946 I was posted to Group Headquarters at Hendon. This was my first 'staff' appointment. There was no available accommodation at Hendon so I got digs at a private house in Harrow, the home of an uncle of my fellow flight commander 'Plug' Lodge. Plug was to follow me to Hendon where we were both 'Operations Staff Officers'. It was interesting that when on duty overnight the ops room became the bedroom for the duty officer and his assistant, who was invariably a WAAF officer. Camp beds were unfolded and made up on each side of the room and in all innocence, when the time came to retire, we did just that!

Whilst at Hendon I paid quite a few visits to various entertainment centres in London, sometimes finishing a late night out by being invited back to a private house. One such occasion led to my meeting the famous French jazz violinist Stéphane Grappelli, who in addition to his skill on the violin was also an accomplished pianist. We had a most delightful musical session with him on the piano whilst I crooned 'Night and Day', one of my great favourites.

In April of 1946 the H.Q. was moved to Milton Earnest in Bedfordshire and it was from there that my romance with Enid was rekindled.

In June I was released from the RAF, total flying hours 3,526. In September 1946 Enid and I were married in her local church at Uppingham.

9. An RAF Commission

In 1946 I was offered a permanent commission in the RAF which, under pressure from my brand new wife and my parents, I turned down. I was, by that time, employed by Cooper, McDougall and Robertson Ltd, the parent company of my father's business, Roxburgh Morgan & Co. The intention was for me to take over from my father in due time. It did not take me long to find out that I was not well suited to civilian life and when the Berlin blockade arose, with the possibility of further hostilities, I decided I had better take up the offer of a permanent commission, which fortunately still stood.

So after a gap of three years I was back in the RAF. On rejoining I was sent to a flying school to be 'refreshed' and then posted to the RAF Central Flying School as a flying instructor. The Central Flying School is the oldest flying training establishment in the world and is where pilots are trained as flying instructors. This was similar to my last job in Canada, but much more advanced and sophisticated. CFS is the very font of flying and one of its many traditions is to provide air displays, the most famous being the Red Arrows. Individual displays also took place and Flight Lieutenant Graham Hulse had a close call when rehearsing for a display in a Meteor jet. He had flown over the airfield at just above ground level at maximum speed, probably close to 500 mph, and pulled up into a steep climb when the Meteor completely disintegrated. By great good luck the cockpit continued to ascend to a good height and on reaching its zenith Graham vacated the cockpit and descended by parachute, completely unscathed. (Round about the same time 'Birdie' Wilson, who subsequently attained the rank of Air Vice-Marshal had a similar experience in a Meteor.)

Graham Hulse was a delightful chap and a brilliant pilot. Soon after this incident he was sent out to the USA for three months to demonstrate the Baliol Trainer. He became so popular in the US that a request was made for him to join the USAF on an exchange posting and thus he joined a Sabre fighter squadron in Korea, where he was shot down. A helicopter almost managed to rescue him but was unable to do so because of the arrival of enemy troops. Graham was captured and never heard of again.

In addition to training instructors, CFS make visits to other training establishments both at home and overseas, including air forces of other nations (upon invitation). These visits include the re-categorisation of individual instructors and the checking of others in order to ensure that standards are being maintained. They are carried out by the Examining Wing, to which I belonged for a short time.

An annual event before the war was the Hendon Air Display where the RAF showed off their skills in the air. One of the best remembered pre-war stunts was a formation of three aircraft performing aerobatics tied together. The only equivalent show to take place since was in 1950 at

Farnborough. As usual CFS made a large contribution, such as a mass formation spelling out 'King George VI' and suchlike. My contribution was a synchronised aerobatics display together with another chap – John Gibbons. We did this in Chipmunks and so were always well within sight of the spectators. (The fast hotrods were often too high or too far away to be seen throughout their acts.) One of our manoeuvres was a side by side spin from about 1,500 feet, recovering at about 500 feet – which on reflection was a bit foolhardy. Sometime later when the Swedish Air Force lost a Chipmunk or two, having failed to recover from spins, De Haviland, the manufacturers asked the Swedish Air Attaché to report that he had seen our display and was in no doubt that recovery from spins had been adequately demonstrated. John Gibbons and I were presented with rather smart shooting sticks by De Haviland for our pains.

A custom dating back to the Hendon Displays was for three of the performing pilots to have tea with the King. Because our display took place fairly early in the show, John and I were two of the three on this Farnborough occasion. Tea was served in a marquee at the back of the Royal Stand and just as I was being handed my cup, which was to be followed by strawberries, Princess Margaret, on noticing that the display interval was over, asked me to return to the viewing area and led me to the front row where we sat down (I had to remove someone's bowler hat and gloves from my armchair in order to comply with the Princess's invitation). The show went on for another hour, after which the fleet of cars approached to take the Royal Party away, at which juncture Air Marshal Sir Ralph Cochrane appeared at my side and asked me for his seat, which I had been occupying for the last hour! Years later when Sir Ralph was dined out of the RAF on his retirement, I reminded him of this incident and he left me rather perplexed when, without comment, he walked off to talk to another group of diners.

The sport of boxing is held in high regard in the RAF and so it was not unusual for requests to be made for the contestants to be fetched from far and wide to play their part in boxing matches. One example of this arose when the Central Flying School, based at Little Rissington in Gloucestershire, was asked to pick up a boxer in Renfrew and deliver him to Hullavington in Wiltshire. I was available to do the job and chose to use a prototype aircraft which we were assessing, made by Avro and called the 'Athena'.[7] The Athena had a nice roomy cockpit with side by side seating for instructor and pupil and visualising that my pugilist passenger would be fairly hefty I drew a suitably adjusted parachute for his use. The weather was bad – thick cloud from 500 feet up to a great height. My flight plan established my cruising height at 5,000 feet and so I was in cloud throughout the journey. During the flight, as was normal, I was 'listening out on my radio' and heard the normal air patter but it was not until getting close to my estimated time of arrival at Renfrew and making my first call that it became clear that my transmissions were not

---

[7] It was in competition with the Bolton Paul Baliol – in the end neither was made in any quantity.

being received. I proceeded to orbit at cruising height in the hope that this unusual pattern would be spotted by an alert Air Traffic Controller and sure enough it was. (It would have been much too chancy to descend through cloud with the cloud base so low.) By a series of heading changes a sort of silent communication was established and although the controller could talk to me and had no way of knowing that Renfrew was my destination, he took me safely down at his base – my old favourite Prestwick.

Whilst the radio was being repaired, arrangements were made to bring my passenger to Prestwick by road, and rather later than would have been desired we set off for Hullavington. A quick call on the radio confirmed that it worked so we continued our journey south, once again in cloud. About two hours later our ETA was getting close but again my calls went unanswered. Orbiting on this occasion produced no offers and bailing out would be an option which was a poor alternative, not least because the boxer had turned out to be a fly-weight and so more than likely if put to the test would fall out of the extended parachute harness I had provided. Luckily, just when things were getting serious, a small hole in the cloud revealed some lights on the ground, which made it reasonably safe to descend and after a few minutes scouting around at about 500 feet – it was getting dark – we spotted an unlit airfield on which we landed. The jolt of the landing caused my radio to reconnect and there were sceptics who doubted whether it had really been out of action. The late hour, the weather, and the darkness ruled out any attempt to continue to Hullavington, which was still twenty miles away, so I regret to say my boxer was prevented from taking part in his bout. Instead we spent the night at some local pub and made our way home the next day.

A naval officer who was a student at the Central Flying School arranged for a few CFS instructors to have a day out in a submarine. A few of us flew down to Lee on Solent one afternoon and were 'dined in' on *Daedalus* and early next morning taken aboard a submarine at Gosport. Needless to say we aviators were filled with trepidation and doubted very much whether we really wanted to be submerged under the sea; in the event it was a most stimulating experience and the sense of destructive power when tracking unsuspecting shipping through the periscope was almost obscene. The discipline during the mock attacks was superb and contrasted sharply with the lack of formality throughout the ship at other times. Late in the afternoon we surfaced somewhere south of the Isle of Wight with the engines out of action, which meant a lengthy delay pending the arrival of a rescue launch.

It had been a great day and we appreciated the dedication and bravery of the submariners – but it turned out to be a strangely specialised bravery because none of the submariners accepted our invitation to come flying with us, all expressing the opinion that it was 'much too risky'!

10. *Lord Trenchard*

For many years after leaving CFS I attended the annual dinners which were held in the CFS mess and preceded by the Annual General Meeting of the Association. At least one member of the Air Council was amongst the several Air Marshals invariably attending these meetings. One year the guest of honour was Marshal of the Royal Air Force, Lord Trenchard. He had been discussing the introduction to the RAF of the 'V' bombers. When he learned that one of the officers present had flown the Vickers Valiant he asked to meet the pilot, who was me. Thus I was taken to the founder of the Royal Air Force to discuss with him this new bomber, which caused me some embarrassment because the great man was very deaf and in no time all those present having tea in the ante-room seemed to be listening to what little I had to say. It was a great honour to be given the opportunity to meet the legendary 'Boom' Trenchard, but under the circumstances, rather un-nerving.

At about the same time the development flying of the Handley Page Victor was nearing completion and Squadron Leader (later Group Captain) Tony Ringer, a one-time member of the CFS Examining Wing, was attached to H. Page to take part in the development programme. On the eve of the H. Page annual staff dinner, Tony and Johnny Alum, the firm's Deputy Chief Test Pilot, carried out one of the strictly planned test flights. Perhaps carried away by the thought of the forthcoming party they deviated from the programme and executed a barrel roll – a quite gentle aerobatic manoeuvre which would not put any undue stress on the aeroplane. Feeling quite pleased with themselves, the two pilots were only too willing to let it be known that they had rolled the Victor. It so happened that the dinner was held at the time of the Suez crisis. Well, when Tony arrived at the party to be greeted by the host, Sir Frederick Handley Page, he was asked if it was true that he and Alum had rolled the prototype Victor. Tony quite proudly confirmed that indeed they had. This brought forth the most severe telling off that Tony had ever experienced, which left him quite un-nerved. He was further ashamed when Sir Frederick asked him if he knew who Nasser's parents were and he had to confess that he did not. Then Sir Fred, who was well known for his knowledge of the bible and his fondness for bawdy jokes, placed a comforting hand on Tony's shoulder and whispered 'two friendly Egyptians' (or words to that effect).

My tour at the Central Flying School based at Rissington in the Cotswolds came to an end following a golf competition in which I was drawn to play against the Air Officer Commanding the group Air Vice-Marshal 'Johnnie' Darvall. He beat me by one hole – a clever tactic on my part perhaps, because shortly afterwards I was promoted to Squadron Leader (again) and posted to Group Headquarters, based at Leighton Buzzard, Bedfordshire, ostensibly as an air staff officer but really as a golf companion for the

AOC. From then on I genuinely tried to beat him and occasionally succeeded.

My duties at HQ were very light and as far as I could tell nobody on the staff seemed to be very busy. This caused me to form the opinion that headquarters served no useful purpose and should be done away with. This opinion was strengthened when, four years later, I was posted to the Air Ministry, which seemed to me to be top heavy and greatly overmanned.

After 18 rather futile months at Group HQ, I got a plum posting of Officer Commanding the Royal Air Force Handling Squadron. When I took over Handling Squadron it was based at RAF Manby in Lincolnshire, the home of the RAF Flying College. We in Handling Squadron were 'lodgers' and reported directly to the Flying Training Directorate at the Air Ministry where my ultimate commander was Air Marshal The Earl of Bandon.

'Paddy' Bandon was an outstanding example of the legendary characters of the RAF. Stories about his exploits, sometimes outrageous, were legion and so I should have been prepared for some surprises when the day came to be visited by him. The Air Marshal came to visit my squadron after spending some time with Air Vice-Marshal Brooks, who was in command of 25 Group, also based at Manby. When the Earl arrived at my office, which had been especially spruced up for the occasion, he sat down and took out a beautiful silver cigarette case and to my surprise did not offer me a cigarette. Instead he took out a half smoked fag, leant towards me, and said 'have you got a light'. This broke the ice nicely and we settled down to a relaxed chat, during which he said he was afraid he had upset AVM Brooks. It was the time of the year for annual reporting on officers (Form 1369) and the Earl, on seeing some of the very detailed character assessment forms on AVM Brooks' desk, passed the remark that submitting these lengthy reports was such a waste of time because, after all was said and done, there were only two types of officer, the 'press-on but lazy' and the 'efficient shits'. The annual reports are, of course, taken very seriously and play a significant role in the careers of officers. Even so, I know of one Wing Commander whose Form 1369 was completed by his Group Commander with the comment 'This officer is a small man with a small mind who has reached his peak'. The said officer was promoted to Group Captain within a few months and eventually retired as an Air Commodore! (I think in this instance it was the reporting officer who was being assessed.)

On one occasion I was at a meeting in Paddy's office at the Air Ministry when Paddy received a phone call. We all heard him say 'Oh yes, I have looked into this, send them to Singapore'. There was a strong feeling amongst those present that he had not given this any thought at all, but as a result hundreds of RAF personnel and their families were sent on their way for a two-year stint in Malaysia.

The RAF Flying College had not been established for more than a year or so when I arrived there. It was conceived as centre of excellence for the further enlightenment of the brightest officers, whose advancement to the highest ranks seemed certain. Places for officers from friendly nations were available, but it was very expensive and most overseas students were from the USA. In fact, the cost of running the college was so high the US claimed that as much as they would have liked to have had an equivalent college in the USA they could not afford it.

Manby was a great place to be lodging and I befriended many officers on the course who, in due time, achieved Air Rank. Some of them became involved in the development of new aircraft and their equipment and were helpful to me in strengthening the connections between the Services and Ferranti Limited by whom I was employed after leaving the RAF.

Air Commodore S.R. Ubee was Commandant. 'Sid' had an outstanding record in the RAF, which he joined on coming home from Canada where, in his young days, he had, amongst other things, helped to build a railroad. He spent some years as a test pilot and was one of the first Commandants of the Empire Test Pilots School. He was easily recognisable by the black eye-patch he wore after losing an eye in an aircraft accident. He left Manby to become Air Officer Commanding 2nd TAF before retiring as an Air Vice Marshal. In retirement he and I and another retired RAF officer, Frank Ellis, built and operated a Ten Pin Bowling Alley in Wokingham, which we sold after 5 years and which is still going strong. Sid did not survive for very long afterwards. He was well into his 80s and crippled with arthritis when he was attacked at his home by intruders, who left him trussed hand and foot. He lay helpless until found 24 hours later.

Air Commodore 'Gus' Walker succeeded AVM Ubee as Commandant of the Flying College. 'Gus' was a legendary figure in the RAF with an outstanding record in the field of sport and in the air. Whilst serving in Bomber Command in the early 1940s he was helping to rescue the crew of a crashed aircraft when an exploding bomb blew off his right arm. Despite his loss of his right arm, Gus continued to fly having made some appendages to his stump which brought flying even helicopters within his scope.[8] Gus went on to become Air Chief Marshal Sir Augustus Walker.

Another of the many illustrious officers at Manby was Andrew Humphrey, who later was my boss at the Air Ministry, where we shared an office. Andrew was one of the few officers to have been awarded the Air Force Cross and two bars amongst other decorations. He rose to the highest when, after being Chief of Air Staff, he was appointed Chief of the Defence Staff. He died whilst still holding this high office.

There was a very disturbing occurrence at Manby when a group of students was en route for a visit to various USA military establishments. They were flying there in a Hast-

---

[8] Gus Walker was Senior Air Staff Officer 4 Group in 1944 when he visited 51 Squadron, in which I was a Flight Commander. At the time I was on crutches, having injured my right foot. Typically, Gus made a beeline for me to express his distress at my plight, no doubt assuming that I had been injured by enemy action. I was deeply embarrassed at having to reveal that my injury was a result of falling off my motorbike. (It is surprising that having been on flying duties throughout the war this was my only injury.)

ings Transport aeroplane commanded by Flight Lieutenant J. Lawrence. These 30 or so hand picked officers were exposed to very real danger when first one and soon after a second of the four engines failed. These failures occurred at a point halfway to the Ascension Islands, and the Captain was forced to turn back towards England, the nearest land. The Controllers at Manby were in constant radio contact with the Hastings, which was steadily losing height and still had about two hours to go to reach Cornwall. News of this crisis quickly spread around the station and the tension was high. After two hours of agony, particularly for the wives, a safe landing was achieved at a Cornish airfield. The loss of this band of potential Air Marshals would indeed have been tragic. I was appointed to conduct the enquiry – I do not remember whether the cause of the failures was established, but I do know that the pilot, Flt Lt John Lawrence, was highly commended for his excellent performance in saving his passengers from a watery grave. John went on to become an Air Vice-Marshal.

This, in a small way, reminds me of an experience I had had years before. Soon after the war, when I was involved with the Stirling after its adaptation to carry some 25 passengers, I was despatched from Stradishall to do an enquiry into a Stirling accident at Balykelly, Northern Ireland. I went over in the station communications aircraft, an Oxford. The hospitality in Ireland was of a high order and when it came time to leave for Stradishall I was very touched to find that the kindness and generosity had extended to piling turkeys and Guinness, crates of the stuff, in my Oxford. It was getting near to Christmas and these gifts would be much appreciated by my fellow men at Stradishall. Off I went, in rather murky weather, and was well on my way across the Irish Sea when one of my engines stopped. Normally this would not have been too serious but as it turned out, owing to my cargo of goodies, the weight was too much for my one good engine and I experienced a rather disturbing loss of altitude. Had I had anybody with me, I would almost certainly have jettisoned enough of my cargo to stop my unwelcome, although slow descent, but luckily the propeller of the failed engine was still wind-milling and at some 500 feet it sprang back into life. (The Oxford's fixed-pitch propellers could not, of course, be feathered, which was just as well; also the fuel and ignition had been left on.) I made a landing at Liverpool's Speke Airport for an engine check but no fault was found, so I carried on with my cargo intact back to a warm welcome. On reflection, all the symptoms suggested that carburettor icing had caused the engine to stop.

I was stationed at Manby and living on the coast at Mablethorpe when the 1952 East Coast floods occurred. The day before the floods I had arrived back from a trip to Cyprus; a range-proving flight in a Shackleton. We had deliberately planned the route for maximum range and had landed at Cyprus 14 hours after leaving Manby – my longest ever flight. One of the four engines had been stopped because of overheating. On inspection, it was found that the coolant pump had a vital part missing. A replacement pump was requested from England, and in due course a pump arrived, but it was the wrong type, so another was sent for. In the meantime the Engineer Officer, suspecting sabotage, had the other 3 pumps removed for inspection. They proved to be OK and the fringe benefit of the whole performance was that my crew and I had a delightful week exploring Cyprus. The return journey was a bit worrying because just as it was getting dark crossing into France near Marseilles, we suffered complete electrical failure. This meant we had no radio and only the mechanical and air driven flight instruments worked. These we illuminated by a hand-held torch. By great good fortune about three hours later, when crossing the English Channel, my Flight Engineer found a way of getting the standby radio to work and we were safely guided back to Manby.

The great floods which affected the east coast of England from Yorkshire to Kent hit Lincolnshire the day after I returned from Cyprus. I had spent the day at home and at about 6pm, went out to fetch the babysitter to enable Enid and me to attend a party at the Station Commander's house at Manby. On my way back with the babysitter I noticed little rivulets of water running down the gutter.

By the time I got back to my house this trickle had turned into a river spanning the width of the road and was deep enough to rise above my exhaust pipe momentarily. In fact, I was lucky to get the car back into my garage. It was obvious that we would not be going to the party, so the next thing was to escort the sitter home. We kitted her up with Wellington boots, but they proved ineffective because on opening the front door the seawater rushed in thigh

high. Undaunted, we waded off into the dark and stormy night (the electricity was off by this time) and had gone about a 100 yards when we heard faint cries from across the road. I left the sitter holding on to the garden railings and crossed over to find an old lady in great distress. I helped her into the nearest house and went back to rejoin my sitter, only to find she had disappeared. (I found out later that she had decided to proceed alone and managed to get to her home safely.) I then decided to return to my house but could not do so because between me and the house there had developed a deep whirlpool, which I judged to be much too dangerous to enter. So off I went in the opposite direction to the main road of Mablethorpe, where I caught up with many other people in search of dry land. Just ahead of me in the dull light I was able to discern a female form made intriguing because, to keep her fur coat from getting soaked she had pulled it high enough to reveal a very shapely backside. This encouraged me to increase my pace but on catching up I was quite touched to find that she was a very, very senior citizen.

Soon I came to the railway station and, finding the platforms to be above water level, along with many others I stayed there for about three hours until, with the tide going out and the storm dying down, and accompanied by another man for safety, we waded back waist-deep towards our houses.

Looking around my house I was amazed to see how the furniture had floated and taken up new positions. On my way upstairs I grabbed a bottle of Cyprus brandy and there was Enid, having got the children to sleep, sitting knitting by candlelight. It was cold and I was wet and there was no hot water, so after a rub down we got into bed, drank a substantial measure of brandy and settled down for the night. We were woken from a deep sleep by loud knocking on the front door to find that a rescue squad was ready to take us to safety (the next high tide would have given problems).

Enid quickly dressed the children in about 6 layers of clothing and off we all went in the back of a 4-ton truck to of Officers Mess at RAF Manby. We were looked after right royally and in due time Enid's parents arrived from Uppingham to take her and the girls back to a place of safety, far from the coast. From then on, until being posted to Boscombe Down, we lived in a much less attractive hiring in Louth.

Whilst at Manby I was quite often visited by old chums, especially those who were in rather boring staff jobs. One of these was Johnny Long, who was said to be deaf to such an extent that is his flying medical category was in jeopardy. It was officially agreed that I should test his ability to hear radio messages whilst airborne. To do this thoroughly we decided to take a Baliol – a side-by-side two-seater trainer aircraft – to Gibraltar, refuelling at Istres (Marseilles) and Algiers, resting at Gibraltar for a day or two and stopping in Paris for a night on our way home (being able to arrange this was one of the great advantages of reporting directly to Air Ministry who were concerned with much more important things than 'special' flights).

Although Johnny was the subject of the test, it was he rather than I who was able to understand the garbled messages we received in foreign accents. I would have had great difficulty in getting through the journey without his hearing acuity, which proved to be excellent. Johnny duly passed his test and retained his flying category.

Another frequent visitor was Wing Commander Dicky Martin, a member of Paddy Bandon's staff who had a vague responsibility for the welfare of Handling Squadron. He and I made courtesy visits to the front line squadrons, spending as much as a week at a time going round 2TAF Stations in Germany in our Athena. These were indeed jolly times. Dicky was a graduate of the Empire Test Pilots School and retired from the RAF to be Chief Test Pilot for the Gloster Aircraft Company, where he completed the development flying of the Javelin. The Javelin was a nice docile aircraft but was rather reluctant to recover from a spin. Dicky carried out dozens of spins in it, trying to establish the best recovery procedure; a demanding task.

On one occasion Flt Lt (later AVM) David Dick, a test pilot at Boscombe Down, failed to recover from a spin and during the descent gave a running commentary of what was going on until bailing out over the Isle of Wight. This was quite a narrow squeak and was an example of demands made on test pilots. Mike Lithgow, who did much of the development flying on Supermarine fighter aircraft, lost his life when carrying out stalling trials on the BAC 111. He got into a deep stall in a nose up attitude from which he could not recover and made a quite slow uncontrolled descent during which he gave a running commentary until crashing. A tail parachute, had it been installed, might have saved him. There was a period during the late 40s and early 50s when many well-known test pilots were killed and many others had close calls.

I suppose the nearest thing we have in the RAF to the sea is our flying boats. I was lucky enough to get the opportunity to fly a Sunderland. The justification was that the 'Pilot's Notes' were due for revision and so I and two of my pilots – Mike Crossley, a pretty famous RN Test Pilot and Flt Lt Short, who had done a tour on Sunderlands – flew down to Pembroke Dock one afternoon and spent the following day flying a Sunderland. It really was such fun for me, starting off by being rowed out to the 'ship' and weighing anchor after getting the engines running. It was interesting to find that the two or three airmen from Pembroke who accompanied us had never been above 1,000 feet and when we declared that we were going up to 5,000 feet to do some stalling tests they pleaded with us to off-load them before this exercise, which we did. (Mike Crossley wrote a book entitled *They Gave Me A Seafire*, an account of his flying career which I strongly recommend to those interested in the Fleet Air Arm.)

A great adventure whilst at Manby was a trip to visit a Venom Squadron in Hong Kong. En-route we would be visiting other squadrons and overseas bases to ensure that our Pilot's Notes were satisfactory. Eight of us, including two associates from the Ministry of Supply, were to make the tour. (Only two of us intended to go initially but the word soon got around and many people offered to come with us.) After much chopping and changing we set off in a Vickers Valetta, loaded with spare parts – including, to my surprise, two spare wheels which took up rather a lot of space in the fuselage. The Station Engineer, Flt Lt Mickey (later Air Chief Marshal Sir Michael) Pringle did a super job in preparing the Valetta for this long journey. A vital member of the team was my most resourceful and versatile F/Sgt (Technical) Dawson. The other tower of strength was my Navigator Flt Lt Ted Brewin, borrowed from the Flying College staff. Ted was most helpful, both in the air and on the ground, and reminded me of my old bomb aimer Chris Smart, who had the same all-round ability and enthusiasm.

We set off from Manby on February 4th 1954. The Valetta had a range of only about 900 miles, so many stops lay ahead. The first of these was Istres (near Marseilles), the home of a French Aeroplane Test Establishment, where we landed in a severe snowstorm. The landing was quite exciting because, try as we may, we could not get the main wheel lights to change from red to green, which suggested that the undercarriage was not fully down. After an initial touch-and-go, which gave the wheels a brief jolt, it seemed to be solid enough so we went round again and with our fingers crossed landed safely with the red lights still showing threateningly. At the end of the runway the resourceful F/Sgt Dawson got out in the snow and fitted undercarriage locks, which enabled us to proceed. We got a great welcome from the CO of one of the Test Units, a very delightful Frenchman who had some time before spent a few days at

Manby with Handling Squadron to study our *modus oper-andi*. We had lunch and on the insistence of our host a sip or two of champagne, and then set off for our next stop, Malta.

The snow was still falling so two French airman led us out to the take-off point, where they then clambered onto the wings armed with brooms and swept the wings clear of snow, whereupon we took off. During our stop at Istres the faulty undercarriage had been examined and declared serviceable so we were disappointed to find on arrival at Malta – quite late in the day – that on selecting undercarriage 'down' the red lights would, again, not go out. Committed to landing we did so again without any trouble. Overnight, whilst we spent the night in the Mess, the undercarriage was once again made 'serviceable'.

The next day we flew to Habbaniya in Iraq via Nicosia Cyprus and on both occasions landed with the undercarriage lights at red – by now we were getting accustomed to this persistent spurious indication. After a night stop at Hab we went on to Maurippur, Karachi, via Sharjar, Iraq. I had visited all these places previously and my recollection of Karachi was one of squalor, poverty and overcrowding. Since my earlier visits the partition of India had taken place and the effect in the city of Karachi was to worsen the situation by at least a factor of four. The RAF unit, however, was comfortably housed and the CO was very kind to us, his visitors. We had a long journey the following day from Karachi to Ceylon via Bombay, two legs of five and a half hours. We made up for this by spending three days with the Ceylonese Air Force, which was then commanded by a seconded RAF officer, Wing Commander Alastair Steadman, whom I had known from our CFS days. (Alastair died quite recently, having retired as Air Marshal Sir Alastair.)

Next stop Changi, Singapore via Car Nicobar, one of a small group of tiny islands in the Indian Ocean which we were very grateful to Ted Brewin for finding it for us after more than four hours flying over a misty sea. We spent three days at Singapore, attending several official meetings, before proceeding to the Philippines, where we were to visit the USAF at Clark Field. We flew there via Labaun in North Borneo, which we were able to explore for a few hours; very memorable and rather beautiful in many ways.

On arrival at Clark Field we were escorted to the 'Officers Club'. The first thing we saw on entering was a long and beckoning bar, where we lingered for some time, listening to a rendering of Glen Miller favourites. Having ordered our steaks whilst at the bar, we went into the dining room to find that the Glen Miller records were, in fact, live music being played by an all-Pilipino orchestra. They seemed to me to be note perfect. The American Officers Clubs were like holiday camps and were used by entire families in multi-coloured clothes, differing hugely from British Officers Mess standards; I prefer the British approach, although on recent visits to RAF messes I have noticed a strong tendency towards US standards.

Our next stop was Hong Kong, but at the time of our visit the weather was unpredictable and could suddenly deteriorate so it was necessary for us to be prepared at the very last minute to return to the Philippines, the only possible diversion, except of course China, where we would not have been well received. The procedure, therefore, was to carry extra fuel (wing tanks in the case of the Valetta), and to listen out for weather reports every fifteen minutes. The flight time was just under four hours and sure enough each weather report was worse than the last, and about ten minutes from our destination, Kai Tak airfield, the message came that it was closed. Luckily, I knew the RAF Wing Commander based at Kai Tak and luckier still he was in the Control Tower. On my appeal he authorised us to divert to Sek Kong (the other RAF base, which is on the New Territories). Our instructions were to fly on a specific course for 6½ minutes,[9] where there might be a break in the clouds enabling us to see Sek Kong, and if so we were to make our own decision on whether to attempt a landing or go back to Clark Field. There was a break and we landed. We spent four days in Hong Kong, attending meetings and sightseeing – how lucky can one get!

We returned to Singapore via Saigon, where we had an hour or so to look around the city, and from Singapore followed our outbound route homewards, except that we called in at El Adem (Libya) en-route from Cyprus to Malta. We landed back at Manby in the early evening on February 24th, having completed 104 hours flying in 19 days.

---

[9] The 6½ minutes were significant because beyond that we would have been over Chinese Territory, which would have been precarious.

The undercarriage lights were still at "red" on our arrival home!

But now to the main function of the Handling Squadron, which is the preparation of 'Pilot's Notes'. The squadron strength was six pilots of wide and varied experience, a single navigator/adjutant, an engineer officer and his 12 technicians, including the worthy Flight Sergeant Dawson. By then I could safely be classed as 'experienced', having flown aircraft of many shapes and sizes in various roles for a total of 4,000 hours. My experience of flying 'jets' however was limited to flying the Meteor whilst at CFS and one flight in a Vampire when on a visit to an old chum, Group Captain Tommy Tomalin, who had been my Chief Instructor at CFS and was then officer commanding North Luffenham, a Vampire Training School. Tommy rose to the rank of Air Commodore and after we had both retired we quite often met in the RAF Club, where I very much enjoyed his company. Apart from a distinguished RAF career, Tommy had, in his younger days, been a champion high diver.

The Meteor got me into trouble once when, on returning to Little Rissington on a training flight, my student selected undercarriage 'down' whilst we were still at high speed. Although I almost instantly selected undercarriage 'up' the damage was done, it had jammed with the port wheel and the nose wheel down and the starboard wheel up. This configuration had not been experienced before and whilst I was doing everything I could think of to rectify the situation, the undercarriage would not budge. Meanwhile, the aircraft controllers on the ground, to whom I had reported my problem, were seeking advice from the Air Ministry and Gloster, the manufacturers, but nobody could think of anything better to do than either take a chance and land or bale out. In the event I decided to land, but during the landing run, whilst still at fairly high speed, the starboard wing could be held up no longer and dropped to the ground; the subsequent violent ground loop twisted the airframe beyond repair. My student and I were helped out unhurt to the loud applause of the many onlookers.

By the time I got to Manby the Meteor and the Vampire were being succeeded by aircraft with considerably higher performance and it was these that I was looking forward to getting my hands on. The first of these was the De Haviland Venom, somewhat similar to the Vampire but sleeker and more powerful. The aeroplane gave me my first taste of the effects of 'compressibility'. Compressibility refers to the pressures building up as the speed of sound approaches, which affect the airflow over the wing, tail and control surfaces. In the case of the Venom, it was possible to reach a speed where all control was lost. The procedure for this was to climb to near maximum height, say, around 40,000 feet and dive at an angle of about 30 degrees at full power. The mach number would creep up to about 0.86, at which point the elevators would become ineffective and recovery from the dive not possible. This, I am sure, sounds terrifying but in fact all was well, because as the descent continued into denser air the indicated airspeed increased and the mach number decreased, thus reducing the compressibility which had been the cause of the loss of control effectiveness. Control progressively returned and the pull out from the dive achieved recovery at about 15,000 feet – wheeeee!

This became known as 'the sixpenny thrill' and all pilots joining a Venom squadron, I am sure, could not wait to experience it. Mind you, there are doubts about the recovery being entirely reliable because of the rare, unexplained dives into the ground.

My next great thrill came with the North America Sabre – the F86A – in which it was possible to exceed the speed of sound. It was not all that easy and required considerable determination in the early models. To get super-sonic it was first necessary to get as high as possible – around 45,000 feet, then roll the aircraft upside down and pull through to vertical dive at full throttle. Once in the dive the mach number would quickly rise to 0.98 and from there on the buffeting would start, but if you put up with this and held the dive you would, with any luck, exceed Mach 1 before the atmosphere got too dense and resulted in an increase in airspeed and a reduction in mach number.

The Hawker Hunter and the Supermarine Swift on the other hand, both of which we handled later, went through the sound barrier smoothly and effortlessly in a shallow dive and super-sonic flight could be sustained for short periods, during which one experienced a wonderful feeling of freedom. Sad to say the Swift was, in a way, my undoing, because of undesirable flying characteristics, which in the end confined its operational use to low-level flying. The troubles arose at high altitudes at high speed. Sometimes in these conditions the engine would stop when making a climbing turn. In air fights this could be a fatal weakness and regrettably no cure could be found. Another nasty feature, and the one which damaged me, was a tendency to stall during turns. These were not ordinary stalls but 'high speed stalls' during which the positive acceleration (G-force) would leap from about 2½G to about 7G, immediately followed by negative G of about 2½. These out of control moments were quite unacceptable operationally and proved to be more than my resistance could stand, resulting in a minor paralysis in my left side which, although it did not immediately restrict me seriously, has worsened over the years to the point where I am now officially disabled. It was a great pity that the Swift which, when in the hands of Mike Lithgow, held the world's speed record, which he relinquished from time to time to Neville Duke in his Hawker Hunter, could not be cured of these defects.

Some years later when at the Air Ministry I was detailed to visit Fairey Aviation at White Waltham to look at a modified Gannet; the modification was the conversion of the navigator's compartment behind the pilot's seat into a pilot's seat with pilot's controls, thus creating a dual control trainer. It was a very challenging conversion because the navigator's seat was much lower than the seat in front and so forward visibility was severely restricted. To overcome this, a periscope was fitted to the rear seat, which gave a forward view over the head of the man in the front seat. With one of the company pilots sitting in the front seat and me in the back we set off on our assessment flight. I found all round visibility was not too bad, but when obliged to use the periscope for the landing I found it to be so aligned that all my attempted landings were about 20 feet above ground and had to be saved from disaster by the company pilot. So it was a case of 'back to the drawing office', from whence I don't think it ever re-emerged.

I frequently attended 'editing' meetings at the Ministry of Defence and more often than not flew to Hendon and then took the tube into town. If travelling alone I enjoyed taking the Avenger on these trips and on one occasion, when my meeting was over, I bought a very expensive (£78) pair of earrings for Enid and felt slightly uneasy about exposing such valuable jewels to what might be a rather unreliable old flying machine. But all went well as I made my way back to Manby in the setting sun.

Another aeroplane which I enjoyed taking on visits was the Fairey Gannet. It always attracted a lot of attention, being the only naval aircraft fitted with two turbo prop engines, each driving its own contra-rotating propellers through a common driveshaft. I enjoyed noting the disbelieving expression on on-lookers faces when they watched the starting procedure, which was to start one of the two engines by firing the in-built starting cartridge and revving it up in order to 'windmill' the second engine into life.

Much as I appreciated my time in Manby, mingling with so many up-and-coming officers, the airfield was too small for the high-performance aeroplanes we were privileged to fly – the longer of the two runways was only 1,400 yards. So at the end of April 1954, after lodging there for two years, the squadron was moved to Boscombe Down, Wiltshire, where, once again, we were 'lodgers'.

Before leaving Manby we did a fly-past of all our current aircraft. These were: Avro Athena, Miles Marathon, Percival Prince, Westland Wyvern (a most unusual and exciting turbo prop), Hawker Sea Hawk (this was one of my great favourites), Supermarine Attacker (not one of my favourites), De Haviland Sea Venom, Gloster Meteor and English Electric Canberra (a wonderfully versatile and successful machine which made many record-breaking flights in the hands of Roland Beaumont and others). What a pity that none of the makers of these still exist. Our six squadron pilots were joined by three others from our landlord unit.

The squadron was 'dined out' in a most splendid way with quite a gathering of VIPs in attendance and after days of preparation and a well-judged intake of alcohol, I was able to make a ten-minute impromptu speech, which, on the encouragement of the assembled diners and the insistence of the Commandant, I completed whilst standing on the beautifully-polished dining table.

Soon after leaving Manby I was awarded the Air Force Cross. This was nice, but I am sorry that none of my fellow pilots were rewarded in any way. They were all excellent pilots, devoted to their quite demanding work and who, by providing the material for Pilot's Notes, greatly simplified the conversion of trained pilots to different types of aircraft and enabled experienced pilots to fly new types of conventional aircraft without further instruction. The Notes could also be carried in the aircraft for ready reference. During my three years we flew some 40 different makes/marks of aeroplane without one reportable incident. This is an indication of the quality of my pilots. They were all well above average – but if I were forced to choose one in particular it would be Lt Mike Crossley RN for his outstanding work on the Westland Wyvern. It was a most complicated machine whose development cost the lives of several test pilots. One of the early weaknesses was that if the many-bladed propellers went into fine pitch they became a more or less solid disc, which created huge drag and rendered the elevators and rudder ineffective. This danger was removed by the introduction of a 'fine pitch stop'. Mike Crossley, after writing the notes, visited the Wyvern squadrons to allay any doubts about this exciting aeroplane, which had had rather a difficult upbringing.

11. *A New Life Beckons*

Boscombe Down, the home of the Aircraft and Armament Experimental Establishment, was an ideal base for Handling Squadron. This was where all aircraft under development were brought in order to confirm the promised performance and to reveal any undesirable characteristics. This involved close co-operation with the aircraft designers and, in particular, with the constructor's test pilots. We in Handling Squadron (sometimes called the 'fumblers') followed on from there, preparing the Pilot's Notes. For this purpose we were allotted one of the early pre-production aircraft, usually the first, to do our work. Being in such close touch with the test squadrons and the company pilots and designers was very helpful. All new service aircraft for the RAF, Fleet Air Arm and Army Air Corps were put through their paces at Boscombe, at their respective test squadrons, and Handling Squadron wrote the Pilot's Notes for all three services, so we could hardly have been in a more suitable place.

The early 1950s were a golden era in British aviation. New types of aircraft were in abundance and technical developments advancing apace. The illustrious aircraft companies were still in being and the company test pilots as famous as film stars. At Boscombe we had visits from Neville Duke and Bill Bedford in their Hawker Hunters and Seahawks, Roly Beaumont in his English Electric Canberras, Ronald Porteous in his Auster, Noel Capper in his Scottish Aviation Pioneers, Brian Trubshaw and Jock Cochrane in the Vickers Valiant and VC10. Roly Falk gave us all a great surge of emotion when he touched down at Boscombe to make the first landing of an Avro Vulcan on completion of its maiden flight. This beautiful delta shape in gleaming white livery was indeed a thrilling sight.

These are just some examples of the many companies and their pilots in being at that time.

And what have we today? British Aero Systems. And what are they making? Mostly, fits and starts in association with our European neighbours.

A very happy social event at Boscombe was the annual golf match against the Aero Golfing Society. The AGS was, and still is, a most prestigious club, the membership being confined to people who have contributed to aviation in some significant capacity. These Boscombe fixtures were a two-day affair and included a dining-in at Boscombe and a dinner at a nearby hotel. During the 36-hole match, bars were set up at about every third hole to ensure that the party spirit was maintained. I am happy to say that on leaving the RAF I became a member of the AGS and still am (an honorary member).

Half-way through my tour, the appointment of Officer Commanding RAF Handling Squadron was upgraded to Wing Commander and so, when my three-year tour came to an end in April 1955, I handed over to my replacement, Wing Commander John Brignell, who had just completed the course at Manby and with whom I had served at CFS. Because my tour had been extended by a year to await the availability of the ideal successor, I was given to believe that when the day came I could more or less choose my next appointment. But this was an illusion and, in fact, I received instructions to take up my appointment at the Air Ministry without further ado. The implication was that the Ministry needed my presence urgently which was, of course, not the case at all.

My appointment was in the Operational Requirements branch with responsibilities in the development of flight instrument systems. This had the great advantage that at least one day a week could justifiably be spent away from the office, attending meetings at the various defence contractors' works. Many of these meetings were to inspect mock-ups of aircraft in the development stages in order to establish locations of instruments and controls and cockpit layouts in general. These I quite enjoyed, and they certainly kept me close to aeroplanes, but inevitably any decisions reached were by committee, which I found to be ponderous. In fact, as I have hinted before, I felt then and still do, that too many people in Headquarters are available to deliberate in committee.

A most attractive feature about being involved in the development of flight instrument systems, in which there were many quite dramatic innovations at that time, was that we in the UK were collaborating with our opposite numbers in the USA. This meant that small teams from both countries exchanged views at 'standardisation' meetings held in the USA at the Pentagon, in Canada at the defence HQ in Ottowa and in London. I attended several of these meetings on both sides of the Atlantic and always included in our team was a famous flying doctor from the Institute of Aviation Medicine, Wing Commander Pat Ruffel-Smith. He was a delightful chap and a very close friend whose flying prowess was such that he was awarded the Air Force Cross and two bars. Pat retired when a Group Captain and was headhunted by an American company, where he continued to make a significant contribution to the new generation of flight instrument systems.

Apart from these escapes into the real world, I strongly disliked my time at the Air Ministry, where I was like a fish out of water. I deeply missed the camaraderie of squadron life, my squadron commander status and my personal service car and driver. To exchange all this for being a very lowly staff officer surrounded by very senior officers who seemed to be preoccupied with self-advancement was an awful come down. Furthermore, travelling to work by train and tube was a serious blow to my morale.

Unsurprisingly then, when I was invited to join Ferranti Limited in their department dealing with aircraft instruments, I jumped at the chance.

My final flight in the RAF was on 7th July 1957, in an Anson returning from Prestwick – where I had been attending a meeting on the Scottish Aviation Prestwick Pioneer cockpit layout – to Hendon. This Anson leaked very badly through the roof and windscreen, so by the time I got to Hendon I was soaking wet. It is strange that my first and last flights in the RAF should have been from Prestwick. My total flying time by then was 4,635 hours and 40 minutes, a far, far cry from my first flight twenty years earlier – 'air experience' – 20 minutes.

Apart from my spell at the Air Ministry I thoroughly enjoyed my time in the RAF. I was so lucky on my return to the service in 1949 to have served at such prestigious establishments as CFS, RAF Flying College and the AAEE Boscombe Down.

I suppose that the Operational Requirements Branch of the Air Ministry could also be considered prestigious. Even so, I have never regretted my decision to leave, especially when I received a 'golden bowler' and a small pension, plus a warm welcome from Ferranti.

I was 39 years old, just the right age to begin a new life.

~ END ~

Poem: To Night

MYSTERIOUS Night! When our first parent knew
Thee, from report divine, and heard thy name,
Did he not tremble for this lovely Frame,
This glorious canopy of Light and Blue?
Yet, 'neath a curtain of translucent dew,

Bathed in the rays of the great setting Flame,
Hesperus, with the Host of Heaven, came,
And lo! Creation widened on Man's view.
Who could have thought such darkness lay concealed
Within thy beams, O Sun! or who could find,

Whilst flower and leaf and insect stood revealed,
That to such countless orbs thou mad'st us blind!
Why do we then shun Death with anxious strife?
If Light can thus deceive, wherefore not Life?

Joseph Blanco White (1775–1841), Irish poet.

From *The Oxford Book of English Verse, 1250–1918.* Sir Arthur Quiller-Couch, ed. (New ed., rev. and enl., 1939) Oxford University Press.

Index

Grange Mouth 1939. Familiar sight at Elementary Flight Training Schools.

Prestwick 1940. Bill Elder, The Author, Ivan Stratham, Bush Richards. Armed and ready to capture enemy parachutists.

No2 EFTS, Prestwick 1939. 'B' Flight office. Ivan Stratham, Bush Richards and Adam Cairns-Smith.

Assiniboia, Saskatchewan 1942. The Author and his Hupmobile in front of the sheriff's house.

Hollywood 1942: supper with Shirley Temple and Doc Frazer at the Brown Derby Restaurant in Vine Street.

Hollywood 1942. The Author taking a dip in Nigel Bruce's swimming pool..

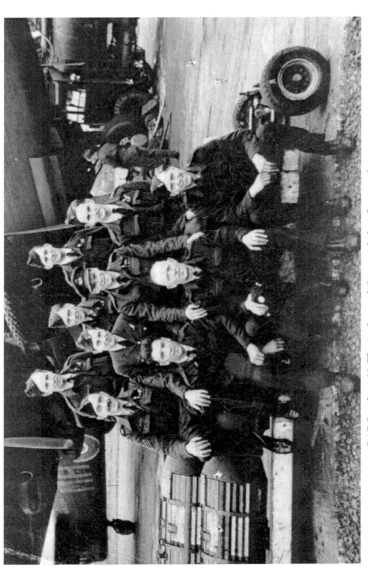

RAF Snaith 1944. The Author and Crew, including fitters and riggers.

Back row: Sgt Jock Meldrum (Mid-Upper Gnr), Sgt Jack Ryde (Flight Engineer) W/O Terry Bennett, RAAF (Wireless Operator)

Middle row: Sgt Gillies Torrence (Rear Gnr), F/O Chris Smart (Bomb Aimer), S/Ldr Ian Roxburgh (Pilot), F/O Jim Robb RNZAF (Navigator)

Front row: Our Groundcrew.

CHELTENHAM CHRONICLE

LEADING ILLUSTRATED PAPER IN GLOUCESTERSHIRE

LARGEST CIRCULATION IN THE COUNTY

EVERY FRIDAY - 2d.

This Picture will appear in the present Week's Issue

1950. De-briefing after air display practice. The Author and Ian Pendred (later Air Chief Marshal)

'The Fumblers' – RAF Manby 1953. John Nicholson, Les Coe, Ian Roxburgh (The Boss), George Turner, Mike Crossley. (Flt/Lt Short, the 6th member of the team, was not available for the photo call).

RAF Manby 1953. Some of Handling Squadron's aircraft.

RAF Manby 1953. Mike Crossley; cockpit familiarisation.

RAF Manby 1953. George Turner drafting Pilot's notes.

RAF Manby 1953. Handling Squadron's farewell flypast before moving to Boscombe Down.